NISTR 7568

NIST
National Institute of
Standards and Technology
U.S. Department of Commerce

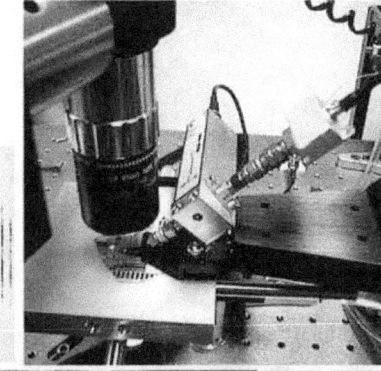

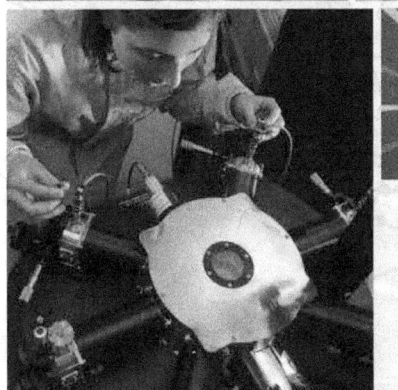

I0437751

Electronics and Electrical Engineering Laboratory

Programs, Activities, and Accomplishments

March 2009

NISTIR 7568

ELECTRONICS AND ELECTRICAL ENGINEERING LABORATORY

U.S. Department of Commerce
Gary Locke, Secretary

National Institute of Standards and Technology
Patrick D. Gallagher, Deputy Director

March 2009

INDEX

This document describes
the technical programs of the
laboratory.

Contact NIST/EEEL,
100 Bureau Drive, MS 8100,
Gaithersburg, MD 20899-8100,
Telephone: (301) 975-2220,
On the Web: www.nist.gov/eeel/

ELECTRONICS AND ELECTRICAL
ENGINEERING LABORATORY AT A GLANCE

One of NIST's Measurement and Standards Laboratories, the Electronics and Electrical Engineering Laboratory (EEEL) conducts research, provides measurement services, and helps set standards in support of: the fundamental and practical physical standards and measurement services for electrical quantities; the fundamental electronic technologies of semiconductors, magnetics, and superconductors; information and communications technologies, such as fiber optics, photonics, microwaves, electronic displays, and electronics manufacturing supply chain collaboration; forensics and security measurement instrumentation; maintaining the quality and integrity of electrical power systems; and the development of nanoscale and microelectromechanical devices. EEEL provides support to law enforcement, corrections, and criminal justice agencies, including homeland security.

Vision

To be the world's leading electromagnetic measurements and standards laboratory.

Mission

To promote U.S. innovation and industrial competitiveness by advancing measurement science, standards, and technology, primarily for the electronics and electrical industries, in ways that enhance economic security and promote our quality of life.

Values

Integrity
...within our organization and in our interactions with our stakeholders

Impact
...through leadership in measurements and standards for our customers and the nation

Excellence
...in all of our undertakings

EEEL consists of four programmatic divisions and two matrix-managed offices:
Office of Law Enforcement Standards
Office of Microelectronics Programs
Semiconductor Electronics Division
Optoelectronics Division
Quantum Electrical Metrology Division
Electromagnetics Division

DIRECTOR'S MESSAGE

The Electronics and Electrical Engineering Laboratory supports U.S. industry by developing measurement science and providing measurement services over the electromagnetic spectrum from DC to light waves. We provide measurements for DC and low-frequency voltage and current, through microwave and terahertz quantities, from infrared to ultraviolet laser power and energy. Our world-class measurement services are supported by research efforts that develop the foundations for tomorrow's measurement sciences, and our talented and dedicated staff members strive to ensure that we are positioned to meet the nation's most important measurement needs.

In this report, you will find that EEEL researchers are developing the world's most advanced sensors, providing advanced gamma-ray imagers for astronomical researchers and single-photon detectors that test the limits of quantum information. Our scientists and engineers are leading the world in a new definition of the kilogram based on electrical units and developing nanophotonics and nanoelectronics measurements to support a new generation of electronic devices. We are creating novel measurements of electrical and optical waveforms that provide frequency, phase, and temporal response at unprecedented accuracy and ever increasing bandwidths and data rates. Our research in bioelectronics is yielding new methods for analyzing DNA, and our efforts in bioimaging will improve the accuracy of magnetic resonance imaging (MRI), thus improving diagnostic capability.

Our work in power electronics and smart grid standards and measurements will improve electrical distribution and address the nation's energy concerns. Our job is to support U.S. innovation by addressing the most pressing electronic and electrical measurement needs, and our staff members take this challenge seriously.

To learn more, please visit our website, www.nist.gov/eeel/. We invite your inquiries and interest in our measurement service offerings, measurement science developments, and opportunities for collaboration.

Kent Rochford, Acting Director

James Othoff, Deputy Director

EEEL STRATEGIC TECHNICAL AREA:
ENERGY

One of the most important issues facing the nation is the need to improve our energy infrastructure to be more flexible, efficient, and reliable while reducing negative environmental impacts. EEEL is building on existing research programs in all of its divisions to better meet this need now and in the future. Our unifying vision is to improve the electric power grid to become a new "Smart Grid," providing a two-way flow of electricity and information. By incorporating distributed computing, communications, and sensors into the power grid to improve its ability to respond to changes, the Smart Grid will become a more robust and innovative energy delivery platform capable of supporting distributed and renewable sources of energy (such as wind, solar, and geothermal) and new products such as plug-in electric vehicles and electrical equipment able to modify energy use in response to external conditions. Under the Energy Independence and Security Act of December 2007, NIST is given a new responsibility to "coordinate the development of a framework ... to achieve interoperability of Smart Grid devices and systems." EEEL is currently leading NIST's efforts to respond to this important and challenging mandate by boldly leading and orchestrating the efforts to develop the comprehensive standards structure necessary for the effective and rapid implementation of Smart Grid technologies. These efforts include engaging a broad range of stakeholders through working groups and workshops, developing a shared vision of interoperability, fully assessing the current standards landscape, accelerating standards development by relevant standards organizations, and recommending standards, policies, or practices to the Federal Energy Regulatory Commission (FERC) once stakeholder consensus is reached.

Metrology development and research in EEEL addresses all facets of our energy vision, including Smart Grid. Our electric power and energy calibrations help to ensure that electric power metering is accurate. Our measurements of power monitoring devices support the ability to monitor the operational state of the power grid in real time to minimize disruptions and outages. To support the Department of Energy (DOE), we have performed electrical efficiency testing for electrical equipment such as power transformers and electric motors. We characterize new electronic materials such as silicon carbide to support their use in advanced high-speed power electronics. Our measurements of superconductors support their use for energy applications such as for higher-capacity power transmission lines. Additionally, our measurements of advanced optoelectronic materials and organic semiconductors and devices support improved-efficiency solid-state lighting and organic photovoltaics. Future work is also envisioned to improve energy generation and storage applications.

EEEL STRATEGIC TECHNICAL AREA:
BIOELECTRONICS

"Bringing the Benefits of Moore's Law to Medicine"

Bioelectronics is a field of research that applies the recent advances in electronics to create medical equipment that will lower the cost of healthcare and improve the way in which doctors diagnosis and treat illness, cancer, and disease. It will provide tools for researchers that will help them to better understand how our bodies work. That knowledge will enable doctors to diagnose medical problems much earlier than they can now, so that treatments can be more effective and less invasive and costly. Electronic technologies have already revolutionized medicine with X-ray and MRI imaging technologies and a long list of other kinds of medical applications including blood pressure measurements, electrocardiograms, and brain activity monitoring. In fact, electronics has become so reliable and ubiquitous in medicine that we don't usually think about how important it has become in the plethora of applications that save lives every day. Bioelectronics will enable new advances in medicine by using the computer-chip technologies that have made processors smaller, faster, and cheaper, and NIST will help make them as commonplace and reliable as going to the doctor's office to take your blood pressure.

Bioelectronics encompasses a range of topics at the interface of biology and electronics, including elements from electronics, biochemistry, biophysics, biomaterials, and bioengineering. One aspect of bioelectronics is the application of electronics to problems in biology and medicine. This includes electronics for detection, characterization, and measurement of biological materials, especially on the molecular, sub-cellular, and cellular level. Another aspect is the application of biological systems and/or processes to create novel electronic components. A third aspect of bioelectronics is based on the interfacing of electronics with biological systems—for example, brain-machine interfacing. Applications in this area include assistive technologies for individuals with brain-related disease or injury, such as paralysis, and artificial retinas.

EEEL has identified and is working on opportunities to develop new molecular and cellular instrumentation tools for systems biology (e.g., metrology for biomolecule detection, identification, and quantification) and new methods to improve the bioelectronic interface (in-vivo electronic/biointerface chips). These include the use of protein nanopores for the detection and quantification of ions, RNA and DNA, proteins, and toxins; the use of single-protein nanopores for aqueous-based mass spectrometry (fig. 1); the use of solid-state nanopores and nanowires for biomarker detection; the ability to manipulate single particles with magnetic traps; the integration of microelectrodes to position cells and to observe growth and toxin response of cell cultures; the integration of microwave heating elements in microfluidic structures to control and cycle temperature (fig. 2); the use of microwave techniques to measure single cell ion channel events with 10 MHz bandwidth; the adaptation of micro-mechanical beams to DNA characterization; and the ability to form disposable chips with integrated electrodes.

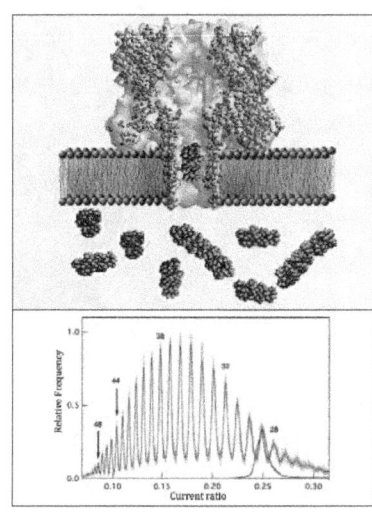

Figure 1. Single-molecule mass spectrometry using electronic nanopore measurements (Robertson et al., PNAS 2008; 104:8207-8211). The entry of individual poly(ethylene glycol) molecules into a single pore (top) causes transient reductions in the ionic current. Larger polymers block the pore conductance more than do smaller ones. Each peak in a histogram of molecule-induced current blockade amplitudes (bottom) corresponds to a particular size molecule in a polydisperse sample. The difference in the length of the molecules that cause successive peaks is 3 Angstroms (red data). The blue trace corresponds to current blockades caused by a monodisperse PEG sample with 29 ethylene glycol repeat units.

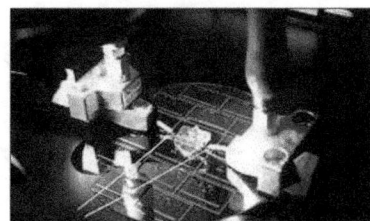

Figure 2. Integration of microwave elements with microfluidic systems for pinpoint temperature control and cycling (Shah et al., J. Micromech. Microeng. 2008; 17: 2224-2230).

EEEL STRATEGIC TECHNICAL AREA:
NANOTECHNOLOGY

Nanotechnology opens new doors to tremendous innovation because material and device behavior is radically different at the nanoscale, allowing new properties and functionalities to emerge, but also creating significant new measurement challenges. Those who can engineer this new functionality into new products and tools will gain tremendous competitive advantage and huge economic and technical rewards. EEEL is developing the nanoengineering measurement infrastructure that is necessary to facilitate the transition of nanotechnology from the lab to the commercial market. EEEL is also harnessing advances in nanotechnology to improve our quantum electrical standards to better tie the U.S. legal electrical standards to the international system of units and to ensure reproducible standard electrical measurements.

Nanotechnology is poised to make a huge difference in the $250 billion semiconductor industry. EEEL is developing metrology that will help enable new nanoelectronic information processing technologies to supplement and/or supplant conventional complementary metal oxide semiconductor (CMOS) devices that are the basis of today's integrated circuits. EEEL has made recent advances in creating test structures and associated test methods for determining the fundamental electrical properties of nanoelectronic components such as Si and GaN nanowire test structures and hybrid molecular/Si test structures. EEEL is developing the tools needed by scientists and engineers to quantify, design, simulate, and manufacture reliability into nanoscale devices. Novel defect characterization techniques have been developed and used to begin to determine the fundamental relationship between materials' properties and nanoelectronic device reliability. New computational state variables other than electronic charge are highly desired in order for future, high-performance information processing devices to reduce the amount of energy per unit area that is necessary for operation. EEEL is making strong efforts to develop the metrology in areas such as spintronics and molecular electronics. EEEL is also making advances in magnetics and optical applications. For example, EEEL has demonstrated single-photon sources and detectors for applications such as novel quantum-based communication systems, quantum computing, and new quantum-based radiometry standards.

Before nanoscale components can fulfill their scientific, technical, and commercial promise, better methods are needed to control their growth, purification, and identification. EEEL has advanced the controlled growth of compound semiconductor quantum dots (InGaAs) and nanowires (GaN) for optoelectronic applications. By utilizing microfluidic methods, EEEL has demonstrated well-controlled nanoparticle formation. Laser-based methods have been utilized for the purification and inexpensive identification of carbon nanotubes. High-performance transistors have been fabricated by the directed assembly of Si nanowires.

Additionally, EEEL is exploiting novel properties in nanotechnological devices to improve our quantum electrical standards. Recent advances have been made in applying Josephson junction technology to improve the capabilities and dissemination of AC and DC voltage standards as well as quantum-based power generation standards. EEEL also is investigating whether the unique properties of graphene — a single layer of carbon atoms — can be harnessed to create better quantum resistance standards and improve the dissemination of the Ohm.

EEEL STRATEGIC TECHNICAL AREA:
SPINTRONICS

Spintronics, which exploits the magnetic spin of the electron instead of its charge, has the potential to revolutionize the microelectronics industry, just as microelectronics revolutionized transistor-based electronics and just as transistors revolutionized vacuum-tube electronics. Future spintronic devices will be 10 times faster, 15 percent the size, and use only about 1 percent of the energy of today's conventional electronics. The goal of the EEEL Spintronics Program is to develop new tools and measurements that bring high-frequency metrology to the nanoscale in order to create "beyond-CMOS" spintronic devices and architectures. The program has three thrusts: metallic spintronics (ferromagnet-based microwave spin-transfer nano-oscillators, spin-transfer magnetic random-access memory (MRAM), spin-wave interconnects, and spin analogs of electronic devices), molecular spintronics (molecular spin-resonance logic, single-molecule/nano-particle spin devices), and the development of a nanoscale workbench (to perform spatially resolved, high-frequency, broadband measurements of active nano-devices).

The growth in computing power is a consequence of smaller electronic devices working at higher frequencies. In charge-based devices, this leads to a significant increase in energy dissipation, which causes chips to get hot. This represents a significant design and performance challenge today, but by 2019 it is expected to halt the dimensional scaling of devices that are based on complementary metal-oxide semiconductors (CMOS). Spintronics could not only solve the heating problem but could combine computer logic with nonvolatile spin-MRAM.

Future applications of this technology include reference oscillators and directional microwave transmitters and receivers in devices such as cell phones and radar systems, wireless chip-to-chip communications, nanoscale clocks, spectrum analyzers, and high-frequency signal processors. Other spintronic devices could be spin batteries, spin diodes and transistors, spin signal mixers, and spin-wave interconnects.

A variety of organic materials have promising spin properties, and molecules can be synthetically tuned at the atomic scale; thus, molecular electronic devices with spin-dependent tunneling transport offer an innovative approach in spintronics. EEEL is developing test structures and methods to determine the fundamental spin-properties of organic materials and assess their use in spintronic devices. Tunneling in a monolayer array of 10,000 molecules between cobalt and nickel electrodes has recently been demonstrated.

The nanoscale workbench will be an advanced metrology tool to measure the high-frequency response of active, nanoscale, spin, and molecular devices. The workbench will combine high spatial resolution with radio-frequency measurements to probe the frequency dependence of defects, the effects of hybridization of atomic energy bands, and environmental factors that can affect device performance. With this tool EEEL will be able to measure spin decay lengths and decoherence times associated with spin currents in real devices and understand the roles of interfaces and structure. The workbench will operate over a broad range of device temperatures using an ultra-high vacuum chamber and four, broadband, scanning probes with tunneling feedback.

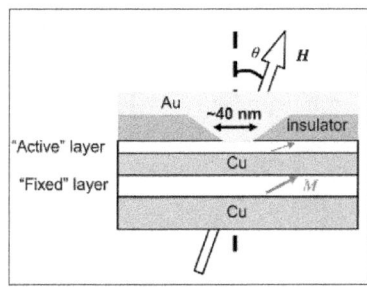

Figure 1: Cross-sectional sketch of a spin-torque nano-oscillator. The two magnetic layers are "active" or "fixed" because of their different thickness and magnetization. A magnetic field H is usually applied at some angle when studying gigahertz excitations in such devices.

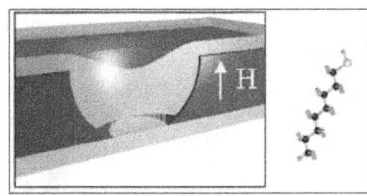

Figure 2: Schematics of a nanopore device with a monolayer of self-assembled molecules and the chemical structure of the octanethiol molecule. The arrow shows the direction of an applied magnetic field.

EEEL STRATEGIC TECHNICAL AREA:
HOMELAND SECURITY

EEEL's role in homeland security began in 1999, when the laboratory's Office of Law Enforcement Standards (OLES) joined the nation's first concerted effort to develop standards for equipment to protect first responders against chemical, biological, radiological, nuclear, and explosive (CBRNE) agents. This experience proved invaluable, and soon after September 11, 2001, OLES was awarded technical leadership of a broad range of programs focused on CBRNE countermeasures.

Today, OLES oversees scores of programs funded by the Department of Homeland Security (DHS). Many of these programs utilize technical resources and expertise within EEEL and elsewhere in NIST. In FY 2008 OLES's homeland security activities brought $25M into NIST, making OLES the recipient of the greatest amount of other agency funding at NIST. In addition, EEEL and OLES partner with DHS and other organizations to identify and address critical homeland security needs, and their personnel serve as key consultants with DHS and chair/serve on dozens of technical committees and working groups.

Recent Accomplishments

- Conducted functional tests of radio-frequency identification (RFID) tags in realistic first responder environments
- Developed and demonstrated software that emergency response organizations can use to verify that their radios conform with the P25 Inter-RF Subsystem Interface (ISSI)
- Developed a detection model that uses dielectric spectra to discriminate between hazardous (acetone, motor oil, bleach) and non-hazardous (apple juice, baby formula, shampoo) liquids

Project Descriptions

The following are a few examples of the exciting homeland security work being done at EEEL:

Performance Metrics and Transmission Standards for RF-Based Emergency Equipment
- Determining how environmental conditions affect the performance of radio frequency-based personal safety systems.

Land Mobile Radio (LMR) Standards and Technologies
- Facilitating development of the suite of standards known as Project 25, which ensures the interoperability of first responder radios made by different manufacturers

Liquid Explosives Detection Standards
- Determining the feasibility of using microwaves to identify explosive liquids in nonmetal containers

Standards for Near Infrared to Radar Frequency Detection of Explosive Devices
- Improving the understanding of explosive devices and their electromagnetic properties

OFFICE OF
LAW ENFORCEMENT STANDARDS

When Congress created NIST's Office of Law Enforcement (OLES) in 1971, no one imagined what it would achieve. A 1960s Presidential Commission had cited "lack of reliable technologies" as a major weakness in the criminal justice and public safety communities, and OLES was chartered to bring NIST's world-class metrology and standards development talents to bear on the crisis. OLES is a program-management organization within EEEL. The office designs and manages standards-development and research projects on behalf of agencies such as the Department of Homeland Security (DHS), the Department of Justice (DOJ), and others. OLES also maintains metrology activities and laboratories for equipment unique to law enforcement, criminal justice agents, and emergency responders.

In FY 2008 the office received approximately $55M from partnerships with the DOJ National Institute of Justice (NIJ) and Community Oriented Policing Services (COPS), and the DHS Science and Technology Directorate and its SAFECOM program. This funding makes OLES NIST's largest source of outside agency (OA) funding. These federal partnerships enable OLES to achieve its mission to develop metrology, standards, and test methods for and support research and development of technologies essential to law enforcement and public safety agencies. Over the years, as the definition of public safety has expanded, so has the Office's expertise.

Major Achievements

OLES began by developing in 1972 the first performance standard and testing program for ballistic body armor – bullet-resistant vests. That effort, which continues today, is credited with saving the lives of more than 3,100 law enforcement officers in the U.S. and countless thousands of law enforcement, corrections, and security personnel worldwide. Yet it was just the beginning.

Over the decades, OLES has:
• developed 300+ standards, equipment guides, and technical reports on technologies ranging from metal detectors and mobile radios to protective gloves and pepper spray;
• developed, beginning two years before September 11, 2001, standards for personal protective equipment for chemical, biological, radiological, nuclear, and explosive (CBRNE) threats – an effort that earned OLES its current position managing the development of performance standards for DHS;
• conducted groundbreaking work in forensic science that has pioneered advances in arson, ballistics, fingerprint, and DNA analyses; and
• expanded its early work on radio technologies into a central role in developing nationwide interoperable communications for emergency responders.

Professionalism and Partnerships

OLES's strengths are its exceptional staff and its partnerships. OLES staff members are recognized experts in a wide range of disciplines. They hold memberships in

Electronics and Electrical Engineering Laboratory

scores of technical and scientific organizations, chair technical and policy-making committees in those organizations, and work closely with the public and private sectors. OLES's partnerships are many – federal agencies, practitioners, academia, industry, non-government standards bodies, and scientific and technical organizations.

Program Descriptions

Below are brief descriptions of some activities underway in the Office's six Program Areas.

Critical Incident Technologies (CIT) deals with technologies essential for rapid first response. Working with DHS, and other federal partners, CIT develops performance standards, test protocols, reference materials and reference data, conformity assessment programs, and guides to help first responders select reliable equipment and services. CIT programs encompass: chemical detectors • radiation and nuclear detectors • X-ray and gamma-ray screening systems • chemical respirators and personal protective equipment (PPE) • chemical and biological (CB) suits and ensembles • decontamination equipment • protective clothing and monitoring systems for firefighters • electronic devices for firefighting environments • urban search and rescue robots • security sensors and sensor networks • radio-frequency (RF)-based security and emergency response equipment • building blast and fire resistance • first responder credentials • latent fingerprint evaluation • and biometric technologies.

Detection, Inspection, and Enforcement Technologies (DIET) expands the use of the electromagnetic spectrum for detecting concealed threats. DIET developed the first metal detector performance standard in the 1970s and has advanced the technology ever since. Today the program explores other segments of the spectrum – from microwave to ultraviolet – for use in security and law enforcement. Current programs focus on standoff detection and imaging of concealed objects • metrology for detection and tracking of individuals behind barriers • RF technologies to capture biometric information such as respiration, heart rate, body motion, and voice • checkpoint detection of metal objects • detectors of hazardous liquids • thermal imaging cameras for firefighters • portable X-ray systems for bomb squads • and complex scene projectors. The program also characterizes weapon performance and is developing a reliable method for testing electroshock weapons such as Tasers.

Forensic Sciences develops tools that enable responders and investigators to gather, handle, and analyze evidence safely and in ways that ensure its integrity in court. The program focuses on: the National Software Reference Library • electronic crime reference data sets and field investigation guides • computer forensic tool testing • fire investigation tools for crime scenes, fire modeling, and burn pattern recognition • Standard Reference Materials (SRMs) for bullets and standards for bullet casings • SRMs for DNA analyses • DNA assays and analysis software • equipment and software validation • and forensic training. The program has also updated essential SRMs for glass refractive index and glass density (needed to calibrate instruments used to analyze glass evidence) and developed a method for enhancing unerased audio on magnetic tape – a significant development in audio forensics.

Public Safety and Security Technologies (PSST) studies chemical-based less-than-lethal technologies, such as pepper spray, and technologies for detecting CB agents and explosives. The program focuses on: reference materials for testing biothreat detection devices and instruments • ability of devices to detect chemical warfare agents and toxic industrial chemicals • field-deployable standard explosive test materials • performance standards for chemical systems such pepper spray and saliva specimens for drug testing • and law enforcement riot gear designed for use in violent situations. PSST also develops CB protection equipment guides with information for evaluating and purchasing safe and reliable equipment.

Public Safety Communications Systems (PSCS) helps to implement a standard nationwide system that enables all law enforcement and public safety agencies to communicate and share data across jurisdictional and technological boundaries. PSCS works with DHS SAFECOM and DOJ COPs to leverage existing standards and requirements, advise IT and wireless standards committees, and evaluate commercial devices that can provide interim interoperability. Through its oversight of the Public Safety Communications Laboratory, PSCS advances interoperability related to: land mobile radios • Voice-over-Internet Protocol • Radio Over Wireless Broadband • interoperability devices • emerging technologies such as SDR, cognitive radio, and MANET • and data exchange. It also conducts studies in fundamental areas such as video and audio quality and RF propagation.

Weapons and Protective Systems (WPS) provides ongoing technical support and research for the NIJ standard for ballistic-resistant body armor. Its evaluation of new materials and ballistic threats, along with its ongoing revisions of the current standard, help ensure continued effectiveness of this key technology. The program also develops and supports standards for other essential equipment, including: stab-resistant body armor • ballistic helmets • bulletproof glass • riot helmets • ballistic shields and plates • vehicle armor • metallic handcuffs • and firearms and holsters.

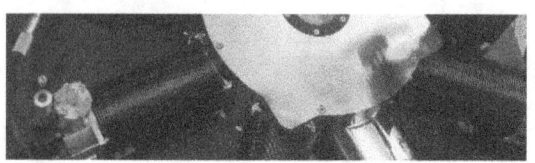

OFFICE OF
MICROELECTRONICS PROGRAMS

The electronics industry, which contributed approximately $7T to the U.S. economy in 2007 and has enabled rapid productivity improvements across multiple high tech sectors, relies on the microelectronics industry for vital components. The microelectronics industry, in turn, relies upon NIST for measurement science and technology to help them meet their own aggressive goals for growth. NIST works closely with industry to develop and apply enabling technology, measurements, and standards to both support today's production and build capability for future technology generations.

Historical Perspective

NIST's predecessor, the National Bureau of Standards (NBS), began work in the mid-1950s to meet the measurement needs of the infant semiconductor industry. While this was initially focused on transistor applications in other government agencies, in the early 1960s the Bureau sought industry guidance from the American Society for Testing and Materials (ASTM) and the U.S. Electronic Industries Association (EIA). ASTM's top priority was the accurate measurement of silicon resistivity. NBS scientists developed a practical nondestructive method 10 times more precise than previous destructive methods. The method is the basis for five industrial standards and for resistivity Standard Reference Materials widely used to calibrate the industry's measurement instruments. The second project, recommended by a panel of EIA experts, addressed the "second breakdown" failure mechanism of transistors. The results of this project have been widely applied, including solving a problem in main engine control responsible for delaying the launch of a space shuttle.

Industrial Metrology Needs

By the late 1980s, NBS (now NIST) recognized that the semiconductor industry was applying a much wider range of science and engineering technology than the existing NIST program was designed to cover. The necessary expertise existed at NIST, but in diverse parts of the organization. In 1991, NIST established the Office of Microelectronics Programs (OMP) to coordinate and fund metrological research and development across the agency and to provide the industry with easy single-point access to NIST's widespread projects. Roadmaps developed by the U.S. Semiconductor Industry Association (SIA) have independently identified the broad technological coverage and growing industrial needs for NIST's semiconductor metrology developments. As the available funding and the scope of the activities grew, the collective technical program became known as the National Semiconductor Metrology Program (NSMP), operated by the OMP.

The NSMP has stimulated a greater interest in semiconductor metrology, motivating most of NIST's laboratories to launch additional projects of their own and to cost-share OMP-funded projects. Most but not all, of OMP's projects are partially funded by the NSMP, which directed a $12 million budget in fiscal year 2008.

Fostering NIST's Relationships with the Industry

NIST's relationships with the SIA, SEMATECH, and its subsidiary, International SEMATECH Manufacturing Initiative (ISMI), and the Semiconductor Research Corporation (SRC) are also coordinated through the OMP. Staff members from OMP and NIST Laboratories represent NIST on the SIA committees that develop the International Technology Roadmap for Semiconductors (ITRS), as well as on numerous SRC Technical Advisory Boards. In 2007, NIST initiated a funding program for the Nanotechnology Research Initiative (NRI) providing $2.8M a year for five years. NRI is a subsidiary of the SRC. NIST staff members are also active in the International Electronics Manufacturers Initiative (iNEMI), the EIA, the International Organization for Standardization (ISO), and Semiconductor Equipment and Materials International (SEMI). NIST supports the U.S. National Committee Technical Advisory Group for the International Electrotechnical Commission Technical Committee TC113 on Nanotechnology Standardization for Electrical and Electronic Products and Systems (Technical Advisor, USNC TAG for IEC TC 113 on nanotechnology) by funding the Technical Advisor to that organization.

NIST supports, together with the SRC, a graduate student at one of the SRC universities. This year the recipient is from the University of Massachusetts at Amherst. He is a student working with Prof. James Watkins at the National Science Foundation (NSF) Center for Hierarchical Manufacturing. The student has already accepted an appointment for the summer of 2009 to work at Intel in Chandler, AZ.

SEMICONDUCTOR
ELECTRONICS DIVISION

The primary mission of the Semiconductor Electronics Division is to provide the measurement and software infrastructure to U.S. industry for mainstream silicon CMOS (complementary metal-oxide semiconductor) and beyond CMOS technologies, as well as other advanced semiconductor technology needs. The division provides necessary measurements, physical standards, and supporting data and technology; associated generic technology; software for improving interoperability; and fundamental research results to industry, government, and academia. Its programs also respond to industry measurement needs related to bioelectronics, microelectromechanical systems (MEMS), power electronics, organic/plastic electronics, and various sub-areas of nanotechnology including nanoelectronics, nanocharacterization, nanoreliability, nanobiotechnology, and nano- and micro-fluidics.

The division has extensive interactions with individual companies, industry organizations, professional societies, and universities; these activities enable the development of a research agenda responsive to the needs of industry and the nation. Active participation in industry roadmapping, such as the Semiconductor Industry Association's International Technology Roadmap for Semiconductors (ITRS), and standards development activities for SEMI are practiced by the division to prioritize and establish programs with the highest potential impact. Division researchers work with SEMI on new standards to help guide the future path of the semiconductor electronics industry in areas such as MEMS, high-k dielectrics, e-diagnostics, e-manufacturing, time synchronization, and traceability. The division helps shape the future direction of semiconductor technology by providing innovative metrology breakthroughs that will propel our industry forward. The division widely disseminates the results of its research, especially in the areas of standardized test methods and Standard Reference Materials (SRMs), through a variety of channels: publications, software, conferences and workshops, and participation in standards organizations and consortia.

The division, with a staff of about 80 including full-time and part-time employees as well as guest researchers, post-doctoral associates, contractors, and students, is based in Gaithersburg, Maryland, and is one of four divisions within the Electronics and Electrical Engineering Laboratory at NIST. The division's technical activities are organized into three groups: the Enabling Devices and ICs Group, the CMOS and Novel Devices Group, and the Electronic Information Group. The division assists industry by providing tools such as new or improved measurement methods, SRMs, test structures and chips, and software that support the needed measurement infrastructure. Division personnel visit industrial sites, host a variety of visitors, and make available tutorial material on an as-needed basis. We also are active in conference and workshop activities that directly benefit the industry.

"Bioelectronics is the discipline resulting from the convergence of biology and electronics and it has the potential to significantly impact many areas important to the nation's economy and well-being, including healthcare and medicine, homeland security, forensics, and protecting the environment and the food supply."

– from A Framework for Bioelectronics: Discovery and Innovation, pg. 1 (Feb. 2009)

POWER DEVICE
AND THERMAL METROLOGY

Summary

Power converters for computers, plug-in electric/hybrid-electric vehicles, alternate/clean power generation, and the advanced power delivery grid rely on the advancement of power semiconductor devices to succeed. Producers of power semiconductor devices want their products to handle higher voltages and temperatures and to operate at higher frequencies, thus enabling power converters with higher efficiencies and lower costs. New semiconductor materials and devices to address these needs are rapidly being developed, but with these new materials and devices come new requirements for characterizing their performance and reliability. The Power Device and Thermal Metrology Project is developing the new electrical and thermal measurement methods and equipment necessary to characterize these devices. This project has played and will continue to play a major role in the growth of the power semiconductor, power electronics, and energy systems industries.

Description

Switch-mode power conversion, using power semiconductor devices and other passive power electronic components, provides the means to convert power from one voltage to another, to convert between direct current (DC) and alternating current (AC) power, and to control motion by delivering electrical power to motor windings or mechanical actuators. As power semiconductor technology has evolved from slow, low-voltage, low-power devices to today's fast, high-voltage, high-power devices, switch mode power conversion has become pervasive and essential in all electrical and electronic equipment except for in the most extreme conditions such as very high-voltage, high-temperature, and cost-sensitive products.

NIST provided the theoretical foundation, measurement methods, and equipment that led to the development and rapid adoption of the most widely used high-power semiconductor device, the Insulated Gate Bipolar Transistor (IGBT). As the IGBT reached its fundamental limits, NIST work began to focus on devices made with new wide-band-gap semiconductor materials such as silicon carbide (SiC) that are beginning to replace conventional devices made with silicon. Power semiconductor devices made with SiC enable operation at higher voltages, higher speeds, and higher temperatures. These new devices are necessary to meet the nation's energy and defense priorities.

The project is addressing a wide range of key issues from methods to monitor material degradation in SiC power semiconductor devices to methods to avoid development of hot spots in microprocessors. The project has pioneered electrical and thermal measurement methods for IGBTs, advanced SiC power devices, and high-density integrated circuits and has transferred these measurement systems to industry. The project is also playing a central role in initiating and leading federal programs to develop advanced power semiconductor devices necessary to meet the nation's power conversion needs for power generation and delivery, advanced naval ship power distribution systems, secure power grids for army main and forward bases, and plug-in hybrid and electric propulsion vehicles.

Major Accomplishments

- Provided leadership, data, theoretical models, and analysis for the DARPA High Power Electronics program necessary to develop the first high voltage SiC power modules and solid state power substation.
- Initiated and led DOE efforts on grid connection of alternate/clean energy sources and identified methods to substantially reduce cost and improve performance and efficiency.
- Developed test structures and methods to determine spatial and temporal resolution of transient thermal microscopes and demonstrating that NIST-developed calibration method provides ten-fold improvement in transient temperature accuracy.

Selected Publications

- A. R. Hefner, "Performance Analysis of 10 kV, 100 A SiC Half-Bridge Power Modules," in Proceedings of the Government Microcircuit Applications and Critical Technology Conference (GOMACTech) 2008 (2008)
- T. H. Duong, J. M. Ortiz-Rodriguez, R. N. Raju, A. R. Hefner, "Electro-Thermal Simulation of a 100 A, 10 kV Half-Bridge SiC MOSFET/JBS Power Module," in Proceedings of the 2008 IEEE Power Electronics Specialists Conference (PESC) (2008)
- A. R. Hefner, "Power Conditioning System Technologies for High-Megawatt Fuel Cell Plants," in 2008 Office of Fossil Energy Fuel Cell Program Annual Report, www.netl.doe.gov/technologies/coalpower/fuelcells/seca/refshelf.html

Figure 1.
Performing high-speed, high-voltage silicon carbide device characterization using NIST-developed, specialized equipment.

Image Copyright Robert Rathe

Contact

Allen Hefner

(301) 975-2071

allen.hefner@nist.gov

MICRO-NANO-TECHNOLOGY (MNT)

Summary

Imagine if your cell phone could test your food for salmonella when an alert was issued by the Centers for Disease Control and Prevention (CDC) or take a drop of your blood, analyze it, and send the results to your doctor when you were sick. Further imagine if it could consult with your doctor about the optimum treatment, manufacture the required drugs, and inject microrobots into your blood stream to deliver the drugs to the organs where they were needed.

This is the promise of the microelectronics revolution as it progresses into the 21st century – even smaller and even more powerful. The goal of this EEEL project is to provide the metrology required to support the evolving micro- and nano-technologies that are the basis for the microelectronics industry's relentless progress as it shifts its emphasis from ever increasing computational power to a diverse set of sensor and actuator applications.

Description

The invention of the integrated circuit in 1959 marked the beginning of the microelectronics revolution. From that date to the present, the primary goal of the microelectronics industry has been to integrate ever-larger numbers of even smaller transistors to produce faster and more powerful integrated-circuit chips. The industry's continued success in achieving this goal has been immortalized in Moore's Law, which requires roughly doubling the number of transistors on state-of-the art computer memory and logic chips every eighteen months. In fact, Moore's Law, which has been incorporated in The International Technology Roadmap for Semi-conductors (ITRS), is the foundation upon which many new technologies were built and many old technologies were dramatically improved. It is no exaggeration to say that these technologies have revolutionized the world in fundamental ways.

Now, a new paradigm, which is adding completely new capabilities to integrated circuit chips, is a rapidly growing component of the microelectronics industry's roadmap. This component, which is often referred to as "More than Moore" to distinguish it from Moore's Law scaling, is based on applying, adapting, and extending the same technology used to produce integrated circuits to include new functionality at the chip level, such as sensors and actuators. This paradigm offers the possibility of creating systems of unprecedented complexity and power, but also introduces new challenges for metrology. Every new function beyond the classical ones of amplification, modulation, demodulation, and filtering requires development of new on-chip measurement capability including appropriate standards.

The activities of the project fall into three major areas. The first area, which is called Standards for Micro Technologies, is addressing the technology and metrology needed to support the integration of microcircuits, microfluidic devices, micro-sensors, and micro-actuators, including the emerging field of microrobotics, which has the potential to revolutionize nano-manufacturing technology and health care. The second major project area, Cellular Bioelectronics Metrology, is focused on the technology and metrology needed to enable a Smart Petri Dish, which will provide highly integrated electronic means to carry out conventional cell culture growth and measurements. The third major project area, Nano Electromechanical Systems, is concerned with developing and applying microfluidic and nanofluidic devices to the formation, characterization, separation, and measurement of nanoparticles, including collaboration on the recent development of a nano-scale glass-blowing technology.

Major Accomplishments

- Developed and demonstrated a single-mask process for fabricating nanofluidic devices with complex out-of-plane topography that will provide improved performance in manipulating and characterizing nanoparticles.
- Developed novel techniques for measuring microhotplate temperature in-situ and demonstrated the long-term repeatability of these techniques that makes them suitable to support Built-in Self-Test (BIST) in microhotplate-based gas sensors.
- Developed and demonstrated liposome nanoparticle formation in microfluidic devices that provides unprecedented control of nanoscale-liposome size and size distribution for innovative drug delivery and nanoparticle environmental health and safety.

Selected Publications

- J. C. Marshall et al., "Young's Modulus Measurements in Standard IC CMOS Processes Using MEMS Test Structures," IEEE Electron Device Letters, Vol. 28, No. 11, pp. 960-963 (2007)
- A. Jahn et al., "Preparation of Nanoparticles by Continuous-Flow Microfluidics," Journal of Nanoparticle Research, Vol. 10, No. 6, pp. 925-934 (2008)
- E. A. Strychalski et al., "Non-Planar Nanofluidic Devices for Single Molecule Analysis

Figure 1.
High Resolution Transmission Electron Microscope (HRTEM) image of a portion of a linewidth test structure showing the atomic planes used to accurately determine the width of the structure.

Figure 2.
Photograph of the NIST micro microwave oven, which is probably the world's smallest.

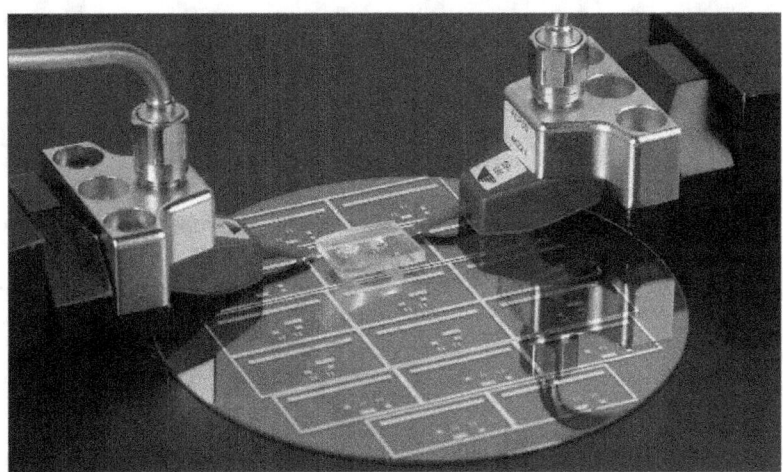

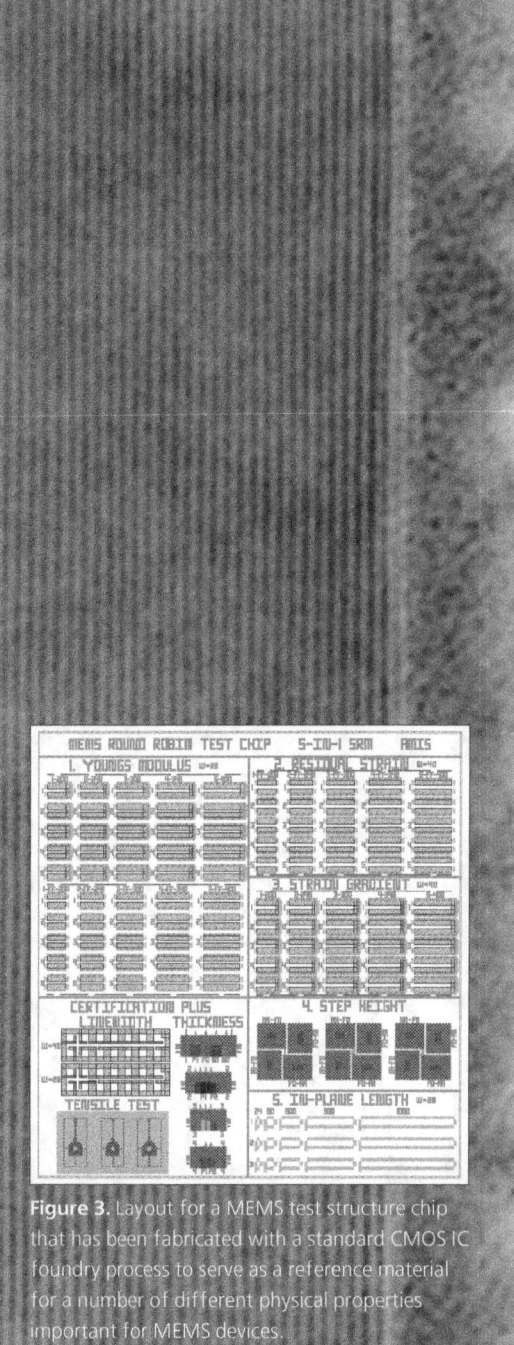

Figure 3. Layout for a MEMS test structure chip that has been fabricated with a standard CMOS IC foundry process to serve as a reference material for a number of different physical properties important for MEMS devices.

Contact

Jon Geist

(301) 975-5484

jon.geist@nist.gov

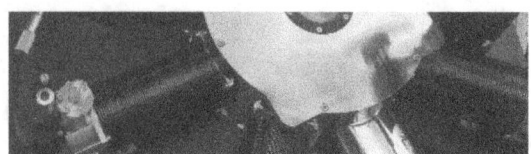

NANOBIOTECHNOLOGY

Summary

Each person, like his or her thumbprint, is unique. However, medicine for disease is distributed to patients as if they are all the same. In the future, in a manner similar to a home blood glucose test, a single drop of blood will allow doctors to accurately prescribe preventative treatment and/or medicine that is tailored to that individual's needs. This new era of personalized medicine will benefit patients directly by correctly identifying and properly treating disease in its early stages. This advance in health care will have an enormous impact on the quality of life. Economic benefits will also be substantial because better therapies will lead to longer and more productive lives and lower health care costs. EEEL's Nanobiotechnology Project is developing technologies that will permit the accurate and simultaneous measurement of many tiny biological molecules that indicate how well our organs and tissues are working and how they respond to treatments.

Description

Over 60 years ago, the ability to make precise and quantitative electronic measurements in living cells made it possible to understand the molecular basis of nerve activity and how single biological molecules work. One of the Nanobiotechnology Project's goals is to take this metrology paradigm to the next level: to combine electronic and optical measurements to address critical needs in health care and homeland security. The methods under development w ll provide a better understanding of complex dynamic processes in cells, organs, and tissues, by detecting, identifying, and quantifying specific biological molecules, including RNA, DNA, proteins, and other biomarkers. This research will lead to integrated microfluidic and microelectronic systems that will be much more powerful than the current generation of blood glucose sensors that revolutionized point-of-care diagnostics for diabetics.

The reductionist paradigm, which has brought about spectacular gains in our understanding of physical and chemical systems, has been applied to biology and culminated with the sequencing of the entire human genome. While powerful, this approach has not provided a complete understanding of how cells and organs work. The new Systems Biology Personalized Medicine approach suggests that the ability to simultaneously detect and quantify many biological molecules (or biomarkers) is essential to understand human wellness and disease. That will require a significant breakthrough in metrology because each human cell can express over 30,000 different proteins and many other types of biomarkers. In addition, because cells and tissues are time-dependent and complex, understanding how therapeutic agents affect them is an open question. Conventional metrologies are not up to this task. Therefore, new systems that can determine the state of a particular patient, and monitor the effect of therapies on his or her health, are needed to achieve the goal of personalized medicine.

Electronics has the potential to address these challenging measurement issues because semiconductor devices can be miniaturized, are scaleable, make use of systems integration, and have the appropriate dynamic and temporal characteristics. Techniques that hold promise, and that are just emerging from the fields of bioelectronics and biophysics, include nanotransducers (nanopores, nanowires), single-molecule optical characterization, and manipulation and isolation approaches (including dielectrophoresis, laser tweezers, and microfluidics). These and related techniques must be further advanced and validated, so that measurements of complex molecular interactions with single molecule sensitivity can be made available to researchers and the healthcare community.

Towards that goal, project staff members are developing new nanoscopic tools for biomarker metrology. For example, researchers have shown that single nanopores can be used to identify and quantify ions, RNA, DNA, proteins, and toxins. They have also demonstrated that similar conductance-based methods can distinguish between molecules that differ in length by only 0.3 nm.

In addition, with scientists in the NCNR, CSTL, and elsewhere, Nanobiotechnology Project staff members are developing methods for determining the structure of integral membrane proteins, which are the principal targets of health-related therapeutic agents. By design, the surfaces used in these studies contain membrane mimics that w ll also serve as a platform for the personalized medicine systems described above.

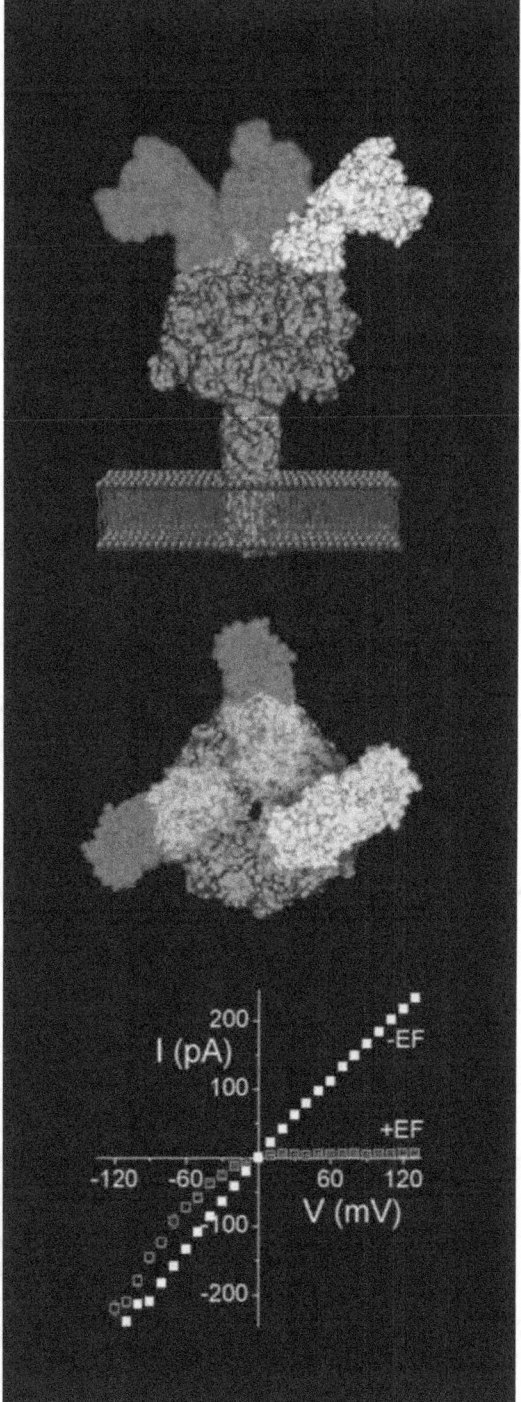

Major Accomplishments

- Developed a new method to determine the structure of membrane proteins, which will help pharmaceutical companies design better drugs for the health care industry.
- Devised an electronic method to measure the interaction between anthrax toxins, which will aid in the development of therapeutics against this biowarfare agent.
- Developed a method to extract single mitochondria from cells, a technique that could prove useful for identifying human remains that are damaged (e.g., in combat or terror attacks) and for determining the cause of certain diseases.
- Invented a conductance-based method to determine the size (or mass) of individual single molecules in solution. This significant advance should enable the electronic detection of many different types of biomarkers simultaneously on a single chip.

Selected Publications

- J. J. Kasianowicz, J. W. F. Robertson, E. R. Chan, J. E. Reiner, V. M. Stanford, "Nanoscopic Porous Sensors," Annual Reviews of Analytical Chemistry 1, 737-766 (2008)
- B. J. Nablo, K. M. Halverson, J. W. F. Robertson, T. L. Nguyen, S. Bavari, R. G. Panchal, R. Gussio, O. V. Krasilnikov, J. J. Kasianowicz, "Probing the Bacillus Anthracis PA63 Channel with Nonelectrolyte Polymers," Biophys. J. 95, 1157-1164 (2008)
- J. W .F. Robertson, C. G. Rodrigues, V. M. Stanford, K. Rubinson, O. V. Krasilnikov, J. J. Kasianowicz, "Single Molecule Mass Spectrometry in Solution Using Solitary Nanopores," Proc. Natl. Acad. Sci (USA) 104, 8207-8222 (2007)

Figure 1.

The binding of Edema Factor toxin (yellow) to a Protective Antigen nanopore (orange) is a critical step in anthrax-induced death and can be monitored electronically. Specifically, the presence of even a trace amount of Edema Factor (EF) can be readily detected because it blocks the current through the pore for positive potentials. EEEL demonstrated that this electronic method could be used to rapidly screen for therapeutic agents to inhibit the interaction of these two toxins. The cell membrane mimic (purple) is 4 nm thick.

Contact

John J. Kasianowicz

(301) 975-5853

john.kasianowicz@nist.gov

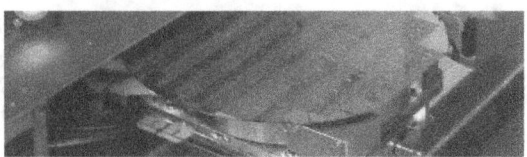

CMOS
DEVICE AND RELIABILITY

Summary

Microelectronics play an increasing role in many critical aspects of our daily lives, including use in airplanes, automobiles, and medical applications. As a result, an electronics failure is increasingly more life-threatening, and reliability assurance is needed now more than ever before. As electronic devices are miniaturized down to the nano scale, reliability assurance is becoming much more complex and challenging due to new degradation mechanisms that come into play as structures get smaller and to the inherent difficulties in measuring such effects in as-manufactured structures. The goal of this project is to develop new test methods, characterization procedures, and models to enable the semiconductor industry to continue to manufacture integrated circuits for reliable electronics and to make the jump into revolutionary new technologies that will present even more severe cross-cutting reliability challenges.

Description

Electronic devices and their reliability have long been important topics of research at NIST. Over the years, NIST has played a central role in this important field. Many of the commonly used test structures and test methodologies in the industry were first developed at NIST. NIST also led many of the national and international standard setting efforts and helped write the testing protocols. Now, industry cannot keep up with the increasing pace of introducing new materials and new device structures into advanced semiconductor technology. Project researchers are responding to industry needs by investigating failure modes and degradation phenomenon in nano scale CMOS (Complimentary Metal Oxide Semiconductor) devices with dimensions as small as 45 nm and "wire" devices with much smaller dimensions. One particular degradation process affects p-channel devices and is extremely difficult to characterize, requiring novel high-speed techniques to capture the full extent of the degradation. A suite of specialized instrumentation is being developed to probe these effects at even higher speeds.

Another phenomenon of concern in extremely small electronic devices is the observation of flicker noise and random fluctuations in a device's operational parameters. Such phenomena can be potential show stoppers. The physical origin of these fluctuations could be the result of only one broken bond or "trap" in the vicinity of the device's channel region. Project researches are using advanced high-speed capture techniques to monitor and analyze the noise and fluctuations over long periods of time. Such data will provide insight into the location and physical origin of the defects responsible.

New material systems such as high-permittivity gate dielectrics and III-V semiconductors are being investigated as possible replacements for silicon-based CMOS technology. Other efforts in the project include characterizing defects in hafnium oxide/indium gallium arsenide devices and understanding their chemical nature. A combination of electrical and optical techniques is being used to determine the band structure and energy barriers in such systems. There is also work in determining the long-term reliability of devices fabricated using silicon carbide. Special high-temperature probe stations capable of heating samples to

400°C were developed to perform time-dependent dielectric breakdown tests on the silicon oxide layer used as the gate dielectric. These data are the first of their kind and are being used to project the lifetime of the devices.

Major Accomplishments

- Developed the world's fastest pulsed current-voltage sweep measurement, achieving a complete high-fidelity sweep of the transistor's operational characteristics in 2 s. This allows stress-induced degradation to be fully measured before it relaxes. These data will help project the lifetime of devices under realistic operating conditions.
- Developed a high-accuracy method for characterizing the bias-temperature-instability phenomenon in MOSFETs (metal-oxide semiconductor field-effect transistors). Such a method is important for industry to be able to obtain accurate parameters for reliability models.
- Discovered a new electron trapping and detrapping mechanism in the negative-bias-temperature-instability of p-MOSFETs that was not comprehended in previous studies. The mechanism helps explain degradation data published in earlier studies.
- Developed a high-speed capture method to obtain and analyze random telegraph signal (RTS) fluctuations in nano-scale CMOS devices. These data suggest that the physical model assumed over the last several decades to explain the origin of the noise is not correct. A new model is being formulated.

Selected Publications

- L. Yu, K. P. Cheung, J. S. Suehle, J. P. Campbell, K. Sheng, A. J. Lelis, S.-H. Ryu, "Channel Hot-Carrier Effect of 4H-SiC MOSFET," European Conference on Silicon Carbide and Related Materials, Barcelona, Spain (2008)
- J. P. Campbell, K. P. Cheung, J. S. Suehle, A. Oates, "Electron Trapping: An Unexpected Mechanism of NBTI and Its Implications," 2008 VLSI Technology Symp., Hawaii, USA, pp. 76-77 (2008)
- J. P. Campbell, K. P. Cheung, J. S. Suehle, A. Oates, "Negative-Bias Temperature Instability Induced Electron Trapping," Appl. Phys. Lett. vol. 93, no. 3, p. 033512 (2008).

Figure 1. Loading 12" wafer containing state-of-the-art CMOS devices into a probe station in preparation of making high-speed measurements of transient changes in device characteristics due to temperature-bias stress.

Figure 2. Panel discussion during the recent Reliability Forum held at NIST. The Forum was jointly sponsored by SRC, NIST, and ISMI. Experts from 32 organizations around the world representing industry, academia, and government participated. The looming crisis in reliability assurance of advanced microelectronics was addressed with a vision for setting future reliability research directions.

Contact

Kin P. Cheung

(301) 975-3093

kin.cheung@nist.gov

MACRO ELECTRONICS

Summary

The concept of electronic paper and wearable electronics used to be a product of science fiction. This futuristic concept for new electronics is closer to reality than most people know and represents a fundamental change in the consumer electronics industry. This is macro electronics – thin, flexible, portable, and cheap – and it promises to revolutionize how people interact with electronics and impact the quality of life. Imagine electronics so cheap that they can be printed directly onto food packaging to give real-time freshness status, or unrolling thin film solar cell arrays to power up temporary shelters. Researchers at EEEL are developing high-impact measurements that investigate the most promising means to enable commercialization of new and diverse macro electronic technologies for a growing list of large-area consumer electronic applications. There is a tremendous commercial market potential for these electronics: printed and organic electronics is a $400M-per-year industry as of 2008, and it is expected to reach $15B per year by 2015.

Description

The Macro Electronics Project was established in 2005 to address metrology gaps that limit or prevent the commercialization of electronics incorporating thin-film active electronic materials and devices. Like silicon in its infancy as a technology, there is much that remains unknown about the electronic, structural, and chemical properties of new materials expected to find use in macro electronic applications. Additionally, there exists a limited understanding of what deleterious extrinsic effects may be introduced during material processing, how to optimize device architecture to minimize parasitic effects that limit the extrinsic electrical performance, and the physical mechanisms responsible for electrical drift phenomena and device failure. Metrology that provides insight to the above allows the rational design of new materials and accelerates the development of computer-aided physics-based tools for macro electronic device design and circuit simulation.

Project researchers initially focused on developing metrology and measurement methodology for thin-film transistors (TFTs) based on solution-processed organic semiconductors (polymeric and small-molecule); a potentially cheap printable technology for flexible electronics. Extensive studies of fundamental charge transport in these novel materials systems allowed the development of physics-based device models that accurately describe the electrical characteristics of transistors. Understanding of macroscale device operation was greatly enhanced by the development of capacitance-voltage measurements and analysis methods as a means to characterizing the electronic properties of the channel region and parasitic contact effects for organic TFTs. Researchers have also demonstrated correlations between molecular design, microstructure, and electronic properties for organic thin film and single crystal field-effect transistors.

Researchers are also developing metrology to enable organic-based photovoltaic devices as a commercially viable technology for providing low-cost renewable energy. Initial emphasis has been placed on developing metrology that will increase the fundamental understanding of photophysical and electronic processes in photovoltaic devices to allow rapid and significant improvements in materials synthesis and device engineering and processing.

Most recently, project researchers in collaboration with Penn State University began addressing metrology gaps that may limit the commercialization of zinc oxide TFTs as a high-performance alternative to hydrogenated amorphous silicon technology (second in economic importance only to single crystal silicon). Zinc oxide TFTs may face a lower entry barrier to manufacturing than organic-based devices given their compatibility with existing semiconductor processing methods, and they may provide significant improvements in electronic performance. Preliminary studies have focused on understanding device reliability and stability, as well as fundamental charge transport and the electronic structure of zinc oxide thin films.

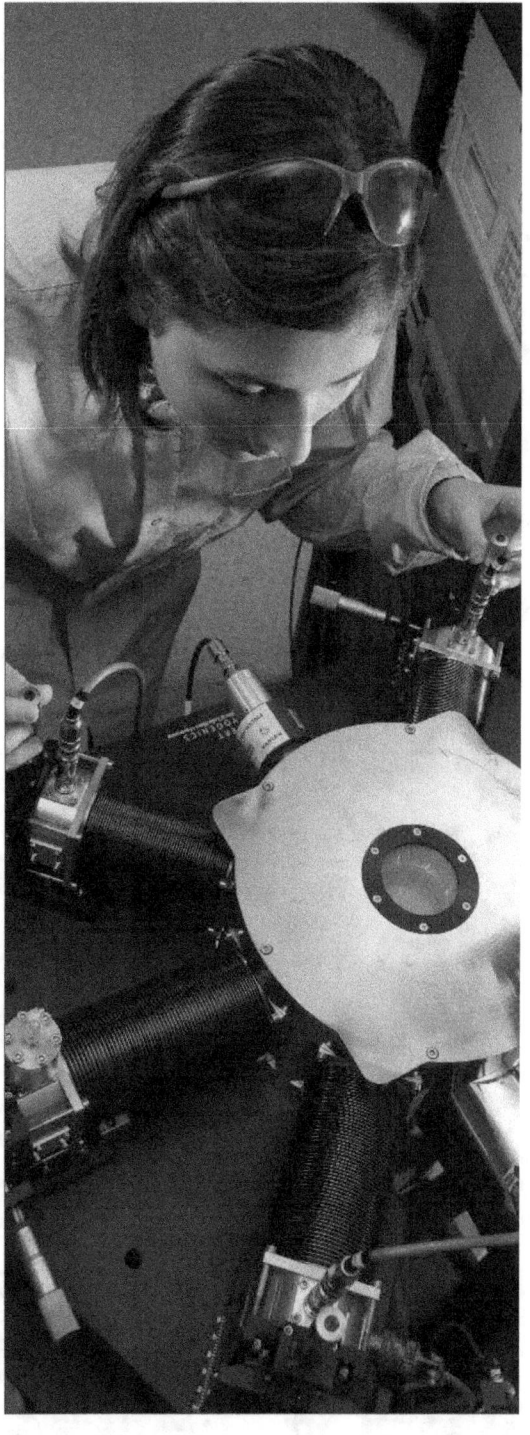

Major Accomplishments

- Developed a novel process for fabricating self-patterned organic thin-film transistors via chemical modification of the electrode interface that simplifies device fabrication and may yield significant reductions in manufacturing costs by eliminating subtractive processing steps.
- Demonstrated the most concrete correlation to date between molecular design, microstructure, and electronic properties for organic thin-film transistors.
- Developed the most advanced capacitance-voltage measurements and analysis techniques for characterizing the contact and channel properties of organic thin-film transistors.

Selected Publications

- D. J. Gundlach, J. E. Royer, S. K. Park, S. Subramanian, O. D. Jurchescu, B. H. Hamadani, A. J. Moad, R. J. Kline, L. C. Teague, O. Kirillov, C. A. Richter, J. G Kushmerick, L. J. Richter, S. R. Parkin, T. N. Jackson, J. E. Anthony, "Contact Induced Crystallinity for High Performance Soluble Acene-Based Transistors," Nature Materials, vol. 7, pp. 216-221 (2008)
- O. D. Jurchescu, B. H. Hamadani, H. D. Xiong, S. K. Park, S. Subramanian, N. M. Zimmerman, J. E. Anthony, T. N. Jackson, D. J. Gundlach, "Correlation Between Microstructure, Electronic Properties and Flicker Noise in Organic Thin Film Transistors," Applied Physics Letters, vol. 92, 132103 (2008)
- B. H. Hamadani, C. A. Richter, J. S. Suehle, D. J. Gundlach, "Insights into the Characterization of Polymer-Based Organic Thin Film Transistors Using Capacitance-Voltage Analysis," Applied Physics Letters, vol. 92, 203303 (2008)

Figure 1.
Characterizing the electronic properties of single-crystal organic field-effect transistors in a vacuum cryogenic probe station.

Image Copyright Robert Rathe

Contact

David J. Gundlach

(301) 975-2048

david.gundlach@nist.gov

NANOELECTRONIC DEVICE
METROLOGY

Summary

More than 60 years ago, the invention of the transistor revolutionized technology for communications, entertainment, transportation, healthcare, manufacturing, and agriculture, as well as national security and defense. The transistor, which is the basic building block of microelectronics, has been scaled to ever smaller sizes until state-of-the-art integrated circuits contain billions of transistors each of which is tens of nanometers in size. Fundamental limitations are being reached for conventional transistors, and novel computing devices capable of replacing it as the logic switch are needed. The Nanoelectronic Device Metrology Project aims to develop innovative measurements and standards that help enable next-generation technologies to develop to the point where commercial applications become feasible. The project is targeting critical tools to assess and speed the development of technologies such as molecular electronics, memristors, organic spintronics, and Si-nanowire transistors.

Description

Throughout its history, the semiconductor industry has constantly aimed to build information-processing devices that deliver higher performance and greater information storage density, while costing less and using less power. Continuation of this trend requires new breakthroughs, and the industry is looking to move beyond the current standard of integrated circuits built using complementary metal-oxide-semiconductor (CMOS) technology.

Current CMOS-based transistors are now considered a type of nanoelectronics, with dimensions of a few dozen nanometers and research ongoing to shrink them further. But right now, the main challenge in moving CMOS forward is making the circuits faster, which involves determining how to regulate their power consumption. Researchers aiming to develop the field of nanoelectronics are therefore investigating ways to exploit the properties of materials at the nanoscale in order to achieve this goal.

EEEL scientists are involved in a wide range of nanoelectronics research. The goal of the Nanoelectronic Device Metrology Project is a fundamental one. Project scientists are developing a total metrology package – a set of new tools, tests, and methods for the nanoelectronics age – that will help nanotechnologies enter the marketplace more quickly. Such a large task is well suited to NIST's uniquely broad expertise and experimental capabilities.

New computational state variables other than electronic charge (such as spin and molecular configuration) are being investigated in order for future, low-power, high-performance information processing devices to reduce the amount of energy per unit area that is required. The project partners with key researcher teams associated with the Nanoelectronics Research Initiative (NRI) to advance this visionary, high-risk area of research.

The project has four major goals: to develop tests and methods to accurately measure the electrical properties of small groups of molecules, ensembles that are the basis of an emerging class of minuscule circuits known as molecular electronics; to develop the metrology for research into silicon-based nanoelectronics; to develop advanced techniques to measure the very small capacitances typical of nanoelectronic

Electronics and Electrical Engineering Laboratory

devices (e.g., nanowire transistors and memristors); and to devise measurement techniques to help with the development of organic spintronics and other alternative technologies.

Major Accomplishments

- Demonstrated that molecular monolayers can be assembled on the same silicon surface (Si (100)) that is used to manufacture today's high-performance integrated circuits, a step toward CMOS-compatible molecular electronics.
- Developed a "directed self-assembly" approach to fabricate high-performance Si nanowire FETs on the wafer scale, demonstrating that self-assembled nanowires can impact large scale integration.
- Combined aspects of molecular electronics and spintronics to design and fabricate a novel device called a "molecular spin-valve." We used a powerful characterization method, inelastic electron tunneling spectroscopy, to study charge and spin transport in this innovative structure.

Selected Publications

- C. A. Richter, H. Xiong, X. Zhu, W. Wang, V. Stanford, W. K. Hong, T. Lee, D. Ioannou, Q. Li, "Metrology for the Electrical Characterization of Semiconductor Nanowires," IEEE Transactions on Electron Devices, Vol. 55, No. 11 (2008)
- N. Gergel-Hackett, C. D. Zangmeister, C. A. Hacker, L. J. Richter, C. A. Richter, "Demonstration of Molecular Assembly on Si (100) for CMOS-Compatible Molecule-Based Electronic Devices," J. Am. Chem. Soc.; (Communication); 130(13) 4259-4261 (2008)
- W. Wang, A. Scott, N. Gergel-Hackett, C. A. Hacker, D. B. Janes, C. A. Richter, "Probing Molecules in Integrated Silicon-Molecule-Metal Junctions by Inelastic Tunneling Spectroscopy," Nano Letters 8 (2), 478-484 (2008)

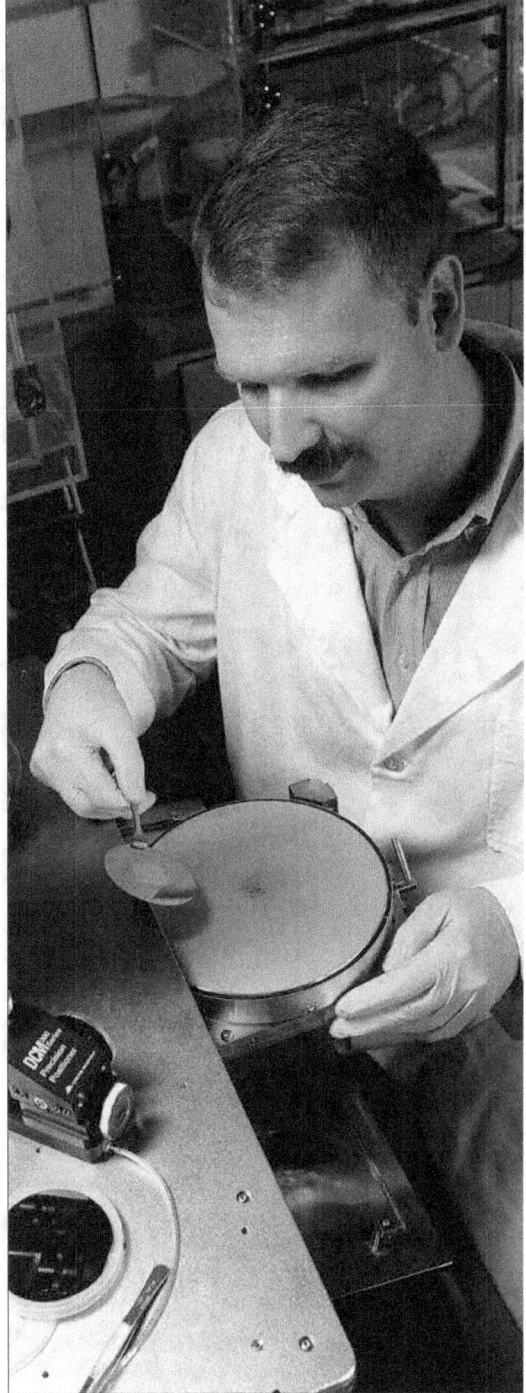

Figure 1.
Loading a molecular electronic sample for electrical characterization.
Image Copyright Robert Rathe

Figure 2. Si-nanowire FET: directed self-assembly.

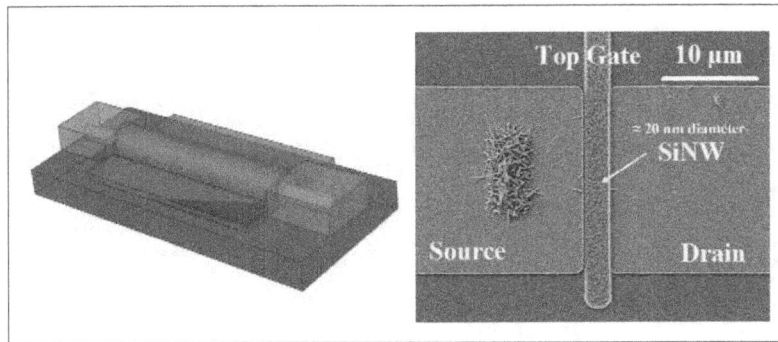

Contact

Curt A. Richter

(301) 975-2082

curt.richter@nist.gov

INFRASTRUCTURE FOR INTEGRATED ELECTRONICS DESIGN AND MANUFACTURING (IIEDM)

Summary

In the tightly interconnected but globally distributed electronics industry, vast amounts of information must flow unimpeded and correctly between industry members in order to create and reliably manufacture the next-generation electronic products. Unfortunately, instead of doing business using a common set of standards, companies, trade consortia, and standards organizations have all created their own standards on how to interact and exchange product information. The result is a tangled mess of competing data exchange standards where there are few if any industry-wide standards, with some even having been created for the sole purpose of giving a particular member an economic advantage. This causes confusion and distrust throughout the industry and impedes commerce. The IIEDM project at NIST is uniquely suited to solving this problem due to its researchers' technical expertise and neutrality, which allows industry consortia, academic institutions, and standards bodies to improve their data exchange standards without concerns of favoritism or bias towards one particular technology or standard.

Description

In the highly competitive global semiconductor and electronics industry, the key to survival for companies is their ability to dramatically increase their pace of innovation, manufacturing, and market share. This is because most electronic products debut as a high profit margin product when first released but rapidly transition down to mere commodity status. Cell phones are a perfect example of this trend where most models typically have a 6 to 18 month shelf life before being made obsolete by newer models. This means that companies typically only have one chance to design, manufacture, and market a new product. Failure on any level (product design flaw, manufacturing process taking too long, product not allowed in target market, etc.) can result in lost sales, profit, and future investments. Few semiconductor and electronics companies can survive failure for long.

Industry knows that the key to surviving this viciously fast product development cycle is the need for information and accurate sharing of data. In designing and producing new products, vast amounts of information need to be exchanged between industry partners. Examples include product design information (necessary to outsource a product's production across multiple companies and multiple countries) and product material composition information (to ensure environmental regulation compliance and market acceptability). Just as importantly as having the ability to exchange information is the requirement that the information exchange is correct and understandable.

If a product's information cannot be exchanged between companies or is accidentally altered in transmission, the entire product can be ruined. What industry needs is a robust IT infrastructure consisting of standards for collaboration, business process integration, and the exchange of technical data. Unfortunately, due to a variety of reasons (lack of coordination across industry, lack of support for standards development efforts, and a lack of trust between business competitors), industry is far from having the uniform set of standards that are needed to achieve their goal of fast data exchange and integration. In fact, with multiple companies, trade consortia, and standards development bodies all working to establish the needed IT infrastructure, industry has been left with a tangled mess of competing standards with no clear idea of which, if any, standard should be used and supported.

Project researchers work with industry to enable the robust IT infrastructure needed to support the electronics industry. Key areas that the project is working on include: the ability to accurately describe electronic components and their attributes, how this data is organized and packaged, and how it is accessed and used through a product's lifecycle (from the product design, through its manufacturing, and, ultimately, to its recycling). Using NIST's reputation for neutrality and technical expertise, the project's researchers are able to increase industry's participation in standards development projects that traditionally no single company will pursue due to its broad-based benefit to industry. In addition, being outside of industry gives this project a unique ability to survey industry activity and guide efforts to avoid overlapping standards development and prevent interoperability problems.

Major Accomplishments

- Provided technical expertise and leadership in the development of IPC 1752, the U.S.'s first material declaration standard, which was created to support efforts to prove compliance with Europe's new restrictions on hazardous materials in electronics. Products failing to comply would be banned from the EU market, negatively impacting the $46 billion dollars of U.S. high-tech exports marketed in Europe.
- Chaired the Information Management Systems chapter of the iNEMI industry roadmapping effort, which seeks to identify future technology roadblocks in managing product information. This allows solutions to be developed and in place by the time needed by industry.

Selected Publications

- E. Simmon, J. Messina, K. Brady, "Information Management for Environmental Concerns," FEO MAGAZINE, No. 2 (2008)
- E. Simmon, J. Messina, "Improving Environmental Information Handling and Data Exchange within the Electronics Industry," Proceedings of 2008 IEEE International Symposium on Electronics and the Environment, San Francisco, CA (2008)
- J. Moyne, Y. S. Li-Baboud, X. Zhu, D. Anand, S. Hussain, "Semiconductor Manufacturing Equipment Data Acquisition Simulation for Timing Performance Analysis," Proceedings of ISPCS 2008 – International IEEE Symposium on Precision Clock Synchronization for Measurement, Control and Communication," Ann Arbor, MI (2008)

Figure 1.
The project brings printed circuit board standards development techniques and technologies to the semiconductor industry

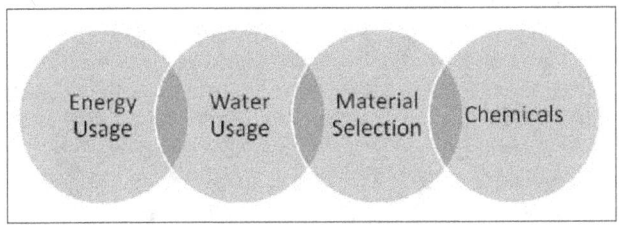

Figure 2.
Regulations will impact multiple areas outside of manufacturing.

Contact

John Messina

(301) 975-4284

john.messina@nist.gov

KNOWLEDGE FACILITATION

Summary

The Knowledge Facilitation Project spearheads the EEEL effort to eliminate paper and to automate manual, labor intensive activities. The project employs cutting-edge web-based technologies to develop custom applications in support of efficient EEEL operations. These applications, which are developed in house and are not available commercially, automate tasks and decrease the administrative requirements of the technical and support staff, while increasing responsiveness to customers and implementing a secure paperless environment. As a result, EEEL scientists are able to spend more time working in their labs than working at their computers to fulfill administrative requirements.

As more and more EEEL data are stored electronically, project staff members have developed ways to share the information through a variety of reporting mechanisms, minimizing the number of times the data have to be entered.

Description

EEEL has taken the lead in developing several IT applications at NIST that help both the researchers and management track the progress a project is making toward meeting its defined goals. The EEEL project database allows researchers to enter milestones, deliverables, tasks, and cost centers by project and to update their status quarterly. Management can use the database to monitor progress without disrupting the researcher, and the researcher can use the database to generate progress reports to outside sponsors. This database is maintained by fiscal year so a history of the project and its milestones and accomplishments is maintained. This application contains all project-related information such as funding, m lestones, staff, progress, etc. for all of the 97 projects in EEEL. Access to the data is provided by user roles; i.e., division chief, group leader, project leader, and staff. Each person's ability to edit information increases based on his or her defined role. This database interacts directly with the NIST publications database to report publications the project has produced. The NIST publications database allows researchers to enter their papers into the editorial review process electronically, and, once the paper is published, the system can make a PDF version of the paper available to the public via the NIST external website with no further action by the researcher required. The project database also interacts with the EEEL trip and talk database to report travel and talks given by project staff. Both of those applications were also developed by the Knowledge Facilitation Project.

Project staff members are also developing an RFID inventory application for EEEL. Inventories cost the division in labor, as the technical staff members spend valuable time locating equipment. By marking each piece of equipment with an RFID tag, coupled with an application developed by project staff, the inventory can be performed by non-technical staff as often as management requests. The cost savings in technical staff time alone is enormous.

With a renewed emphasis on safety, project staff members are developing a safety database to store information about hazards located in each researcher's laboratory. The database will store information about lasers, high voltage, etc., and it will automatically print warning signs for the laboratory doors. Hazard reports by building and floor will be easily generated, so management can verify safety procedures during quarterly safety inspections. Project staff members are committed to helping the researchers spend more time in the lab.

Major Accomplishments

- Developed a web-based application in JAVA to initiate, store, and manage the workflow process for all NIST publications. This EEEL application was so successful, it was adopted NIST wide.
- Developed the Information System to Support Calibrations (ISSC), which is a structured-query language database-driven application. The ISSC stores all of the administrative, technical, and financial data involved with items calibrated at NIST.
- Developed a scheduling and accounting system for the NIST AML Nanofabrication Facility. It allows researchers to schedule time on equipment in the Nanofab and charges them by the time the facility was used.
- Developed and demonstrated a prototype inventory application, using RFID technology, for inventory control for EEEL. This will ultimately free researchers from having to do time-consuming inventory assessments.
- Developed follow-on application to the ISSC to manage internal NIST calibration data.

Selected Software Applications

- Electronic Project Database
- OLES Body Armor Database
- EEEL Solvency
- Personnel Database
- Trip Database
- Bibliography Database
- RFID Inventory Database
- Cost Center Database
- Check Standards Database

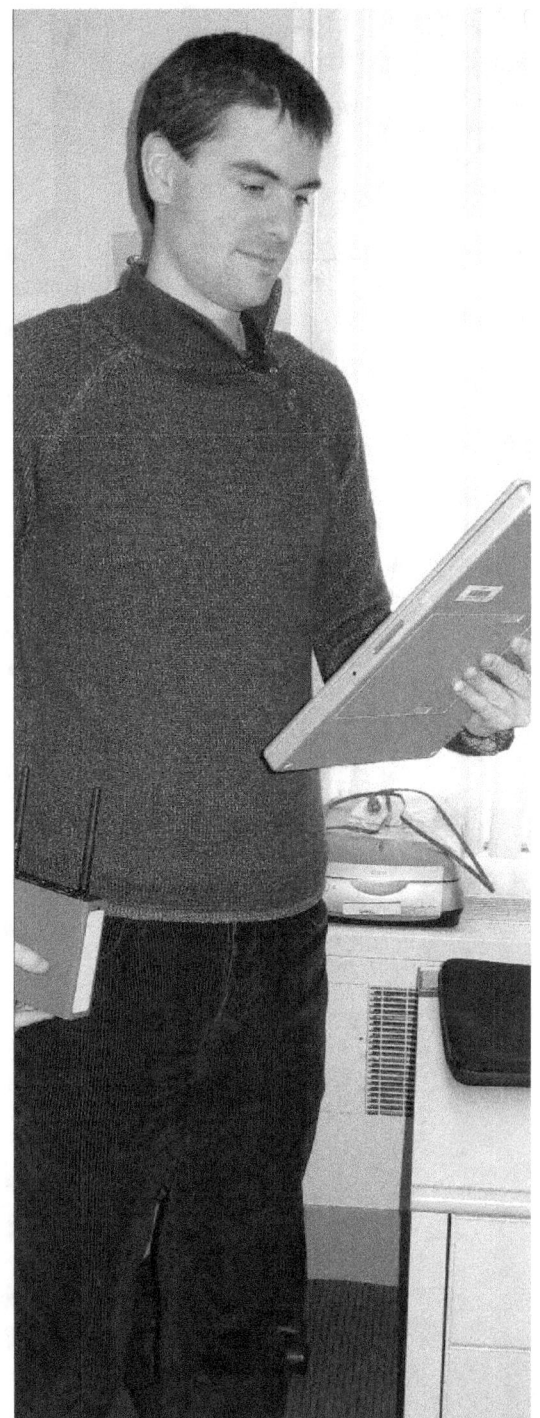

Figure 1.
Using RFID Technology for equipment inventory.

Contact

Kevin Brady

(301) 975-3644

kbrady@nist.gov

OPTOELECTRONICS
DIVISION

Optoelectronics is the study of electronic devices that produce, detect, and control light. The mission of the Optoelectronics Division is to provide the optoelectronics industry and its suppliers and customers with comprehensive and technically advanced measurement capabilities and standards, as well as traceability to those standards. We take metrology seriously. In optoelectronics, as in many other fields, metrology is a key part of the industrial infrastructure that establishes competitiveness. Consistently specified products are essential in fair trade, and measurements are a key element in efficient manufacturing. The cost of measurements often ranges between 10 % and 30 % of the cost of producing a product. Advancing the field of optoelectronics metrology is therefore an important task.

The division is comprised of eight projects focused on four major areas: radiometry, telecommunications, quantum optics, and nanophotonics. Our activities are well-aligned with the national and NIST priorities of measurements and technology for energy, environment, manufacturing, healthcare, physical infrastructure, and information technology. Our focus on a small number of significant technical areas enables us to maximize impact and benefit from collaboration among the projects made possible by our common optoelectronic technology focus.

The division maintains the U.S. national standards for laser power and energy measurements and uses them to provide the broadest range of laser calibration capabilities available anywhere. Each year we perform over 200 calibrations of power- or energy-measuring instruments for more than 50 customers. We also provide artifact calibration standards called Standard Reference Materials. These components provide customers with the capability of performing periodic instrument calibrations traceable to national standards in their own laboratories. We also develop solutions for tomorrow's critical measurement challenges in nanoscale optoelectronics, the creation and characterization of engineered photon states, quantum information, and optical communications.

The division is well-connected with both public and private stakeholders. We maintain close contact with the optoelectronics industry through major industry associations, such as the Optoelectronics Industry Development Association (OIDA). We also directly gather input from and assist customers in companies and universities. With collaborators, we lead fundamental research in areas such as fiber sources for next-generation atomic clocks, single photonics for ultra-secure communications, and carbon nanotubes for state-of-the-art detector coatings. We also transfer detector technology, trace gas sensing methodology, and other research to the public sector. Finally, we represent NIST to the major domestic and international standards-developing organizations active in optoelectronics − especially the American National Standards Institute (ANSI), the International Electrotechnical Commission (IEC), the International Organization for Standardization (ISO), and the Telecommunications Industry Association (TIA) − and provide impartial technical expertise in their negotiations.

Our intent is to be the preeminent source of optoelectronics metrology in the world. We strive to provide the best optoelectronic measurement services possible and perform the research and development that best enhances measurement sciences in optoelectronics.

DISPLAY METROLOGY

Summary

Televisions, computers, and telecommunications equipment are merging into advanced systems that enable unforeseen applications in many areas, such as education (remote learning), entertainment (3D movies), and medicine (remote surgery). Displays are everywhere – thermal imagers for firefighters, airplane cockpits, and your doctor's office. To facilitate worldwide commerce in displays, methods for characterizing display quality are needed to ensure that a display will work under the available lighting conditions – ranging from daylight for cell phone users to smoky buildings for firefighters. To ensure equity in the marketplace, NIST is working with industry to develop standards and the necessary measurement tools to characterize displays under a wide variety of conditions.

Description

The United States is a major user of electronic displays for medical, automotive, avionics, consumer, and computational use. The first three applications require stringent testing to ensure adequate performance for viewing and interpreting digital images. For example, medical radiologists require displays that will provide accurate contrast and resolution of digital images; correct medical diagnoses depend upon it. In addition, well-defined methods for specification and verification of display quality are necessary to enable worldwide commerce of displays. Sound metrology tools are urgently needed in this highly competitive environment of new and emerging display technologies to ensure quantitative metrics for comparing the performance of emerging technologies. Further, universally recognized and accepted standard documents are needed to provide customers with the necessary knowledge to make informed purchases for their applications.

To address these needs, EEEL has focused on developing a common set of best practices in critical measurement areas. These areas include reflection metrology and stray light management (veiling glare, ambient contributions) and the development of transfer standards and devices to facilitate direct comparisons of different display technologies under different lighting conditions – from the brilliant daylight in an airplane cockpit to the dark automobile interior at night.

In the area of reflection metrology, EEEL researchers have developed quantitative methods based upon the bidirectional reflectance distribution function. They are using a three-component reflection model of specular (with a distinct virtual image proportional to the luminance of the source), Lambertian (perfectly diffuse, luminance proportional to the illuminance), and haze (a diffuse intermediate state of between specular and Lambertian that is peaked in the specular direction but proportional to the illuminance). EEEL is extending these techniques to address issues related to daylight readability of displays.

Major Accomplishments

- Developed world-class short course on display metrology. Other NMIs send their staff to NIST to learn about best practices.
- Developed methods for characterizing luminance probes for use with high-contrast medical displays, critical for clinical diagnostics.
- Published popular consumer guide for purchasing flat panel televisions, featured in *Home Theater Magazine*.
- Led international standards activities; e.g., SID International Committee for Display Metrology.

Selected Publications

- E. Kelley, M. Lindfors, J. Penczek, "Display Daylight Ambient Contrast Measurement Methods and Daylight Readability," J. Soc. Inf. Display 14, 1019-1030 (2006)
- J. B. Dinaburg, F. Amon, A. Hamins, P. Boynton, "Performance of Liquid-Crystal Displays for Fire-Service Thermal-Imaging Cameras," J. Soc. Inf. Display 16, 703 (2008)
- M. Dowell and E. Kelley, "Tricks of the Trade: Tips for Buying Flat Panel Display Televisions," NCSLI Metrologist, 28-29 (2008)

Figure 1.
Reflection measurement apparatus for large flat panel displays. Reflection measurements are critical to the evaluation of display performance under ambient illumination conditions, which can vary from blue sky illumination on a cell phone to the reflected light from office walls onto a desktop monitor.

Figure 2. Multi-sun-level photoluminescence measurement apparatus under calibration.

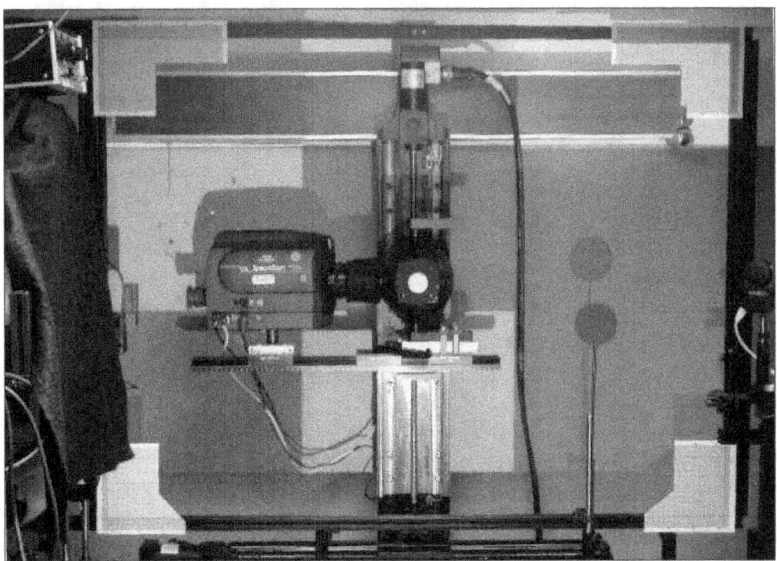

Contacts

Edward Kelley
Paul Boynton

(301) 975-3014

paul.boynton@nist.gov

LASER RADIOMETRY

Summary

Accurate characterization of lasers is important to applications such as communications, medicine, and semiconductor manufacturing, as well as laser safety. This project focuses on measurements of critical laser parameters, especially laser power and energy. Project staff members participate in national and international standards committees for laser safety and optoelectronic devices. Through research into new optical materials and detectors, the Optoelectronics Division has extended and improved measurements of lasers and optical detectors, including development of low-noise, spectrally flat, highly uniform optical detectors; high-accuracy transfer standards for optical-fiber and laser power measurements; and advanced laser systems for laser power and energy measurements.

Description

Meeting the current and future needs of the laser and optoelectronics industries requires investigation and development of improved measurement methods and instrumentation for high-accuracy laser metrology over a wide range of powers, energies, and wavelengths. The Optoelectronics Division has historically used electrically calibrated laser calorimeters to provide traceability to the SI units for laser power and energy. The division has also developed measurement capabilities based on a Laser Optimized Cryogenic Radiometer, which provides an order of magnitude in accuracy improvement for laser power measurements, compared to electrically calibrated radio-meters.

With few exceptions, all of the primary measurement standards for establishing traceability to fundamental units for radiometry are based on thermal detectors. Research into optical coatings has led to superior thermal detectors with absorber coatings consisting of purified carbon nanotubes. To support advanced carbon nanotube coatings, project staff members have developed a set of characterization tools for practical measurements of bulk nanomaterials using non-contact probes pioneered at NIST. Existing measurement tools are neither practical nor useful for current and future large-scale production of nanomaterials. These tools often rely on physical contact between the test probe and the material under study. However, physical contact between probes and nanomaterials may alter the material property of interest; e.g., differentiating bulk resistance from contact resistance. Advanced, cost-effective analytical techniques are needed so that manufacturers, product developers, and regulatory agencies can truly "see" what they have. Photons, being massless and chargeless, are an ideal, non-contact probe. These non-contact techniques, relying on photon-matter interactions, include resonant-coupled photo-conductive decay, high-Q dielectric measurements, absorption spectroscopy, and fluorescence.

Major Accomplishments

- Completed international comparisons of laser power with Germany, Great Britain, Japan, Mexico, Russia, and Switzerland.
- Demonstrated a novel optical detector with spectral response variations less than 1 % over a wavelength range from 600 nm to 1800 nm.
- Published absolute reflectance and absorbance values of carbon nanotube films, critical for international documentary standards and as input to commercial product development.
- Developed critical metrology for high-efficiency, laser-based manufacturing processes.

Selected Publications

- J. Lehman, K. Hurst, A. Dillon, A. M. Radojevic, R. M. Osgood, "Multiwall Carbon Nanotube Absorber on a Thin Film Pyroelectric Detector," Opt. Lett. 32, 772-774 (2007)
- Vayshenker, J. Lehman, D. Livigni, X. Li, K. Amemiya, D. Fukuda, S. Mukai, S. Kimura, M. Endo, J. Morel, A. Gambon, "Trilateral Optical Powermeter Comparison Between NIST, NMIJ/AIST, and METAS," Appl. Opt. Lett 46, 643-646 (2007)
- K. Ramadurai, C. L. Cromer, J. H. Lehman, K. E. Hurst, L. A Lewis, A. C. Dillon, R. J. Mahajan, "Evaluation of Thermal Threshold of Carbon Nanotubes for Thermal Detector Coatings," J. Appl. Phys. 103, 013103 (2008)

Figure 1.

Photograph (right) and scanning electron microscope images (left) of a thin-film pyroelectric detector coated with multi-walled carbon nanotubes. We have observed that multi-walled carbon nanotubes are superior to single-wall carbon nanotubes for a thermal absorber having high absorption efficiency, high damage threshold over a broad wavelength range. (Lehman et al., Opt. Letts., 32, 772-774 (2007).

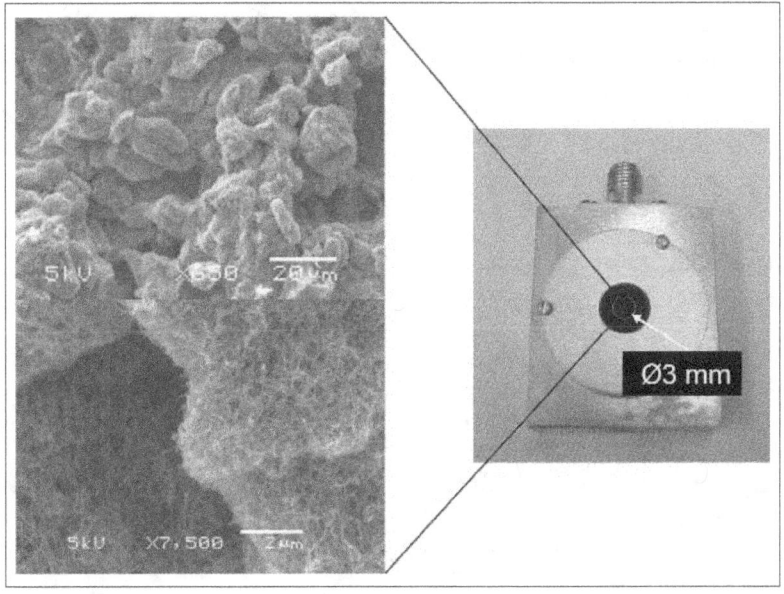

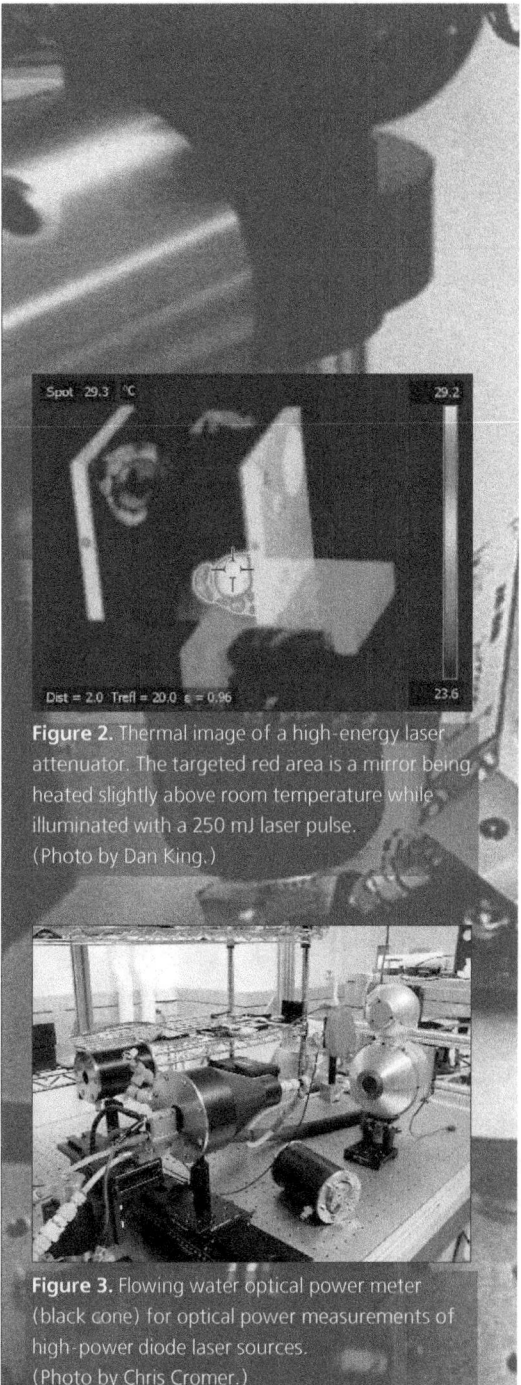

Figure 2. Thermal image of a high-energy laser attenuator. The targeted red area is a mirror being heated slightly above room temperature while illuminated with a 250 mJ laser pulse. (Photo by Dan King.)

Figure 3. Flowing water optical power meter (black cone) for optical power measurements of high-power diode laser sources. (Photo by Chris Cromer.)

Contact

John Lehman

(301) 497-3654

john.lehman@nist.gov

HIGH-SPEED
MEASUREMENTS

Summary

E-mail, Web searches, text messages, bank transfers, landline phone calls, even wireless calls all spend time as pulses of light flashing through fiber-optic lines spanning tens, hundreds, or thousands of miles. Today's economy relies on these forms of high-speed communications, and NIST plays a crucial role in providing the means to test the equipment on which these communications depend by developing novel methods for calibrating optical and electrical waveforms. These methods will enable the design and qualification of current and next-generation communication networks that is required to achieve the goal of true broadband access in every American community.

Description

Optoelectronic communications hardware translates electric currents into light waves and back again at a pace that can move data as fast as 40 gigabits per second — a speed great enough to transmit full-length digital movies across the country in something over a second. EEEL has pioneered the high-speed measurement standards and methods crucial to the functioning of high-speed communication equipment as well as other vital radar, remote sensing, wireless communications, and computer-networking hardware. Through a combination of electro-optic sampling (EOS) and covariance-based uncertainty analysis, EEEL calibrates high-speed photodiodes to be used as electrical pulse generators for characterizing high-speed test equipment in both time- and frequency-domains.

The covariance analysis creates a framework for maintaining the correlations in the uncertainties of the frequency-domain impedance measurements and mismatch corrections in the EOS measurements so that uncertainties in the time-domain can also be determined. An important application of these calibrated pulse generators is the calibration of oscilloscopes and other high-speed temporal waveform measurement systems used in the digital electronics, wireless communications, and fiber optic communications industries. When combined with the NIST Timebase Correction Software, engineers can overcome some of the bandwidth limitations of their test equipment, enabling product specifications with known uncertainties rather than the current practice of placing upper limits on signal accuracy, leading to needlessly large tolerances in high-speed components and systems.

With the prospect of faster all-optical switching equipment, engineers will need a way of measuring light-signal quality, understanding its inevitable degradation, and dynamically compensating for such impairments in the equipment sending the original signal. To this end, EEEL is measuring light signal quality as well as various forms of signal degradation in work indispensable to next-generation all-optical networking.

Major Accomplishments

- Developed first traceable electro-optic sampling system to calibrate photodiodes up to 110 GHz.
- Demonstrated world's only calibrated complex frequency response and time-domain impulse response with mismatch corrections and full point-by-point uncertainty analysis in both time and frequency domains thus enabling traceability to new classes of high-speed devices.
- Created publicly available software to correct for both random and systematic timebase errors in high-speed sampling oscilloscopes.

Selected Publications

- J. A. Jargon, X. Wu, and A. E. Willner, "Optical Performance Monitoring Using Artificial Neural Networks Trained with Eye-Diagram Parameters," IEEE Photon. Technol. Lett., vol. 21, pp. 54-56 (2009)
- P. D. Hale, D. F. Williams, A. Dienstfrey, C. M. Wang, A. Lewandowski, T. S. Clement, D. A. Keenan, "Complete Waveform Characterization at NIST," Conference on Precision Electromagnetic Measurements, June 8-13, 2008, pp. 680-681 (2008)
- D. F. Williams, A. Lewandowski, T. S. Clement, C. M. Wang, P. D. Hale, J. M. Morgan, D. A. Keenan, and A. Dienstfrey, "Covariance-Based Uncertainty Analysis of the NIST Electro-Optic Sampling System," IEEE Trans. Microwave Theory Tech., vol. 54, pp. 481-491 (2006)

Figure 1. Graphical representation of the correlation matrix corresponding to systematic errors in measuring the waveform of Figure 1. Light areas show times that are highly correlated with each other, while dark areas show times that are only partially correlated. Knowledge of the covariance matrix, which is closely related to the correlation matrix, allows transformation of the uncertainty between the time and frequency domains, when appropriate. The technique for transforming the uncertainty was developed at NIST.

Figure 2. A digital optical communications signal measured with linear optical sampling. The gray dots are an "eye" diagram of the signal, which has a four-level phase-sift keying format, dominated by random noise. The colored dots are obtained by waveform averaging the eye diagram with a precision time base to reveal individual signal trajectories, allowing signal distortions to be distinguished from noise.

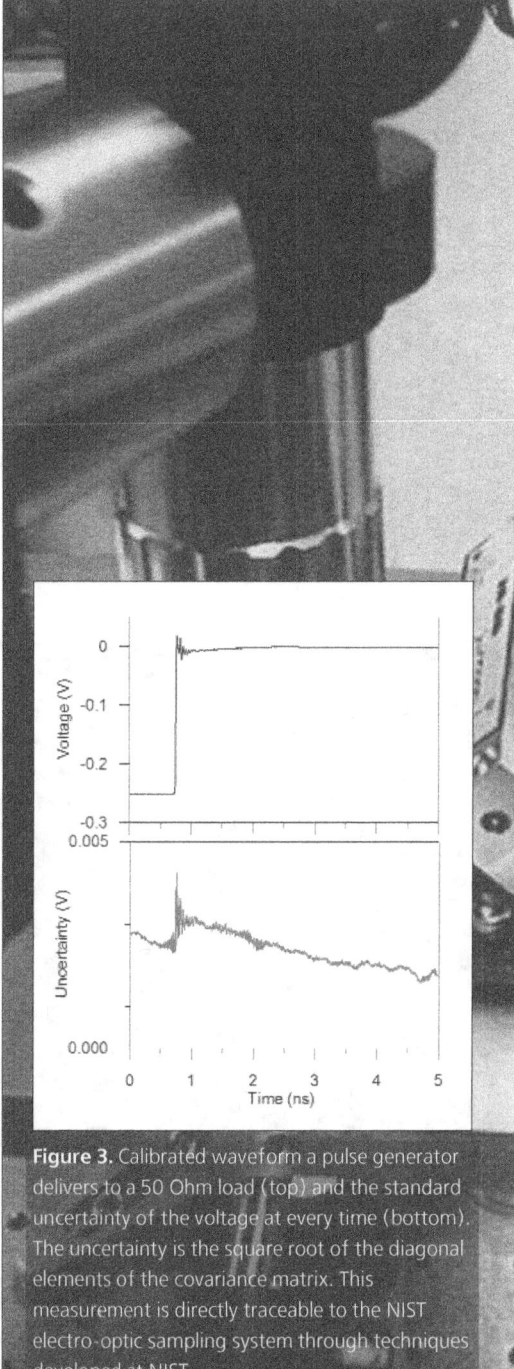

Figure 3. Calibrated waveform a pulse generator delivers to a 50 Ohm load (top) and the standard uncertainty of the voltage at every time (bottom). The uncertainty is the square root of the diagonal elements of the covariance matrix. This measurement is directly traceable to the NIST electro-optic sampling system through techniques developed at NIST.

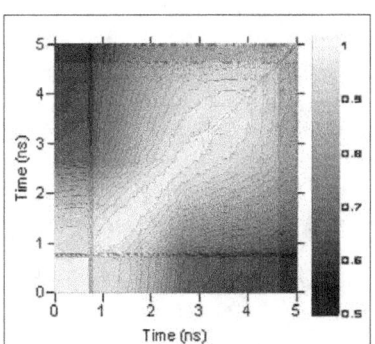

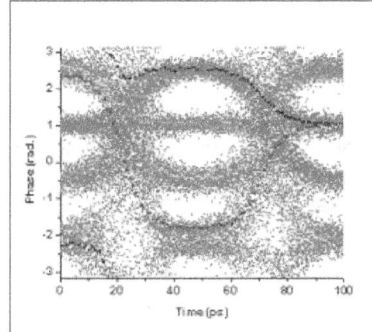

Contact

Paul Hale

(301) 497-5367

paul.hale@nist.gov

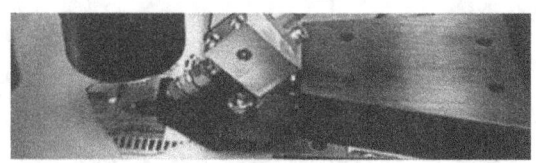

FIBER SOURCES AND
APPLICATIONS

Summary

Optical frequency combs convert a laser source containing a single frequency of light into pulses that include thousands of frequencies. This project aims to develop frequency comb technology for a growing list of applications.

Using a comb working at optical telecommunications wavelengths, project physicists have transmitted signals from next-generation optical atomic clocks across hundreds of kilometers. They have demonstrated how pairs of combs working together can increase by a factor of one hundred the speed of trace chemical analysis with significant enhancements in sensitivity. Frequency combs also promise to enable extremely accurate distance measurements and to assess the quality of high-speed telecommunications signals with unprecedented precision.

Description

In 2005, NIST scientist John L. Hall shared the Nobel Prize in physics for his part in the invention of the optical frequency comb. In the frequency domain, the output of a frequency comb is literally a comb of narrow, sub-hertz, optical lines, while, in the time domain, the output is a highly coherent pulse train with sub-femtosecond timing jitter. The original comb relied on a titanium-sapphire laser, but, in the last five years, scientists in this project and elsewhere have built combs using much less expensive commercial fiber-optic telecommunications components and are exploring the promise of using economical devices to improve timekeeping, chemical analysis, precision ranging, and telecommunication diagnostics.

Working with the NIST Time and Frequency Division, project scientists have demonstrated that fiber-laser based frequency combs can support measurements of the highest performance optical clocks at fractional frequency uncertainties below one part in 10^{17}. At these uncertainties, current satellite transmission methods are inadequate; however, project scientists have demonstrated that it is possible to transmit these highly stable signals over 250 km of standard optical fiber, as a first step to a nationwide fiber-optic distribution of clock signals.

EEEL scientists also have begun to explore other applications that could benefit from the uniquely coherent and broadband output of these comb sources. In the area of spectroscopy, they have measured the coherent optical response of a molecular gas over 15 THz of optical bandwidth. In laser ranging, they have demonstrated micrometer-level ranging at kilometer distances in millisecond timescales. This rapid absolute ranging could support large-scale manufacturing or the future formation flying of satellite arrays. Finally, in the area of telecommunications, project scientists have demonstrated high-resolution measurements of high-speed phase-modulated waveforms. Such measurements could provide novel diagnostic capabilities in next-generation high-speed telecommunications.

Major Accomplishments

- Developed first self-referenced phase-locked fiber-based frequency comb source in the 1100 nm to 2200 nm wavelength region to support the most advanced optical clocks.
- Demonstrated coherent transfer of high-frequency stability optical signals over 250 km of fiber with a fractional stability of 3×10^{-16} at 1 s.
- Expanded potential applications of fiber frequency combs by demonstrating high-resolution molecular spectroscopy, ranging, and characterization of telecomm modulators.

Selected Publications

- I. Coddington, W. Swann, N. R. Newbury, "Coherent, Multiheterodyne Spectroscopy Using Stabilized Optical Frequency Combs," Phys. Rev. Lett., Vol. 100, No. 013902, pp. 013902-1-013902-4 (2008)
- P. Williams, T. Dennis, I. Coddington, W. Swann, N. R. Newbury, "Vector Characterization of High-Speed Components Using Linear Optical Sampling with Milliradian Resolution," accepted for publication in IEEE Photonics Technology Letters.
- N. R. Newbury, P. Williams, W. Swann, "Coherent Transfer of an Optical Carrier over 251 km," Opt. Lett., Vol. 32, No. 21, pp. 3056-3058 (2007)

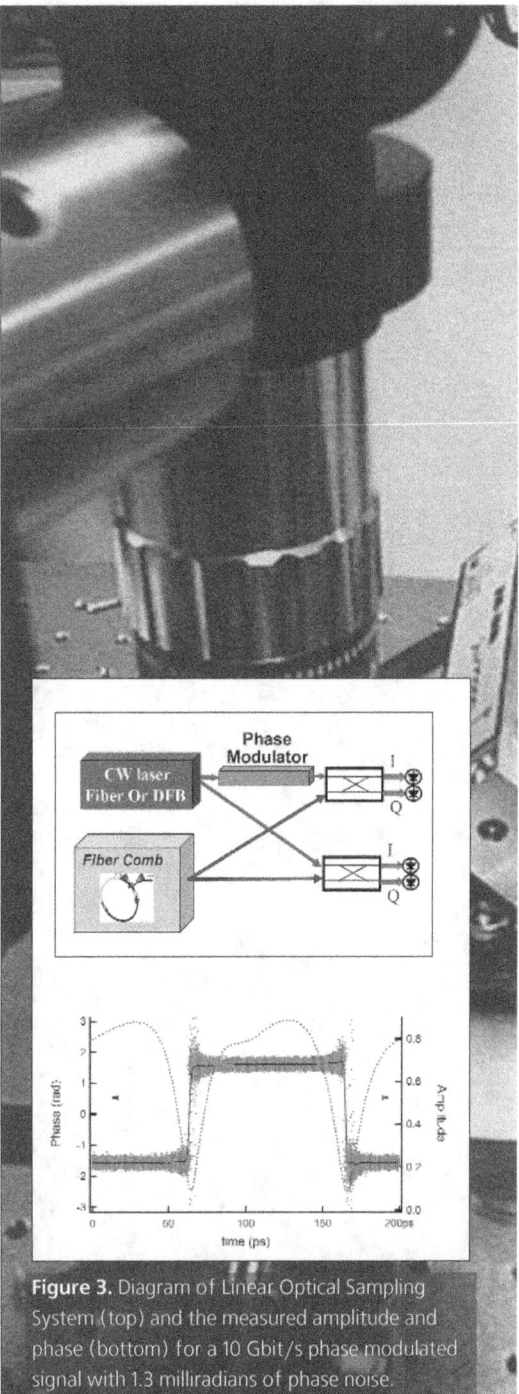

Figure 3. Diagram of Linear Optical Sampling System (top) and the measured amplitude and phase (bottom) for a 10 Gbit/s phase modulated signal with 1.3 milliradians of phase noise.

Figure 1. Optical response of hydrogen cyanide (HCN) molecules. Image was obtained directly in the radio-frequency domain by mixing the signals from two fiber combs, one of which passes through the HCN sample and the other serving as a reference.

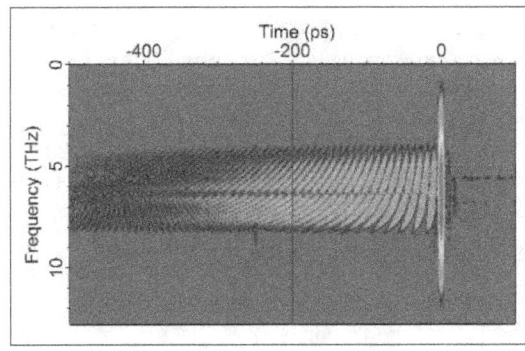

Figure 2. The light traveled a total of 251 km, 76 km around installed fiber in the Boulder Research and Administration Network (red line) and 175 km on spooled fiber maintained at NIST. Using an optical feedback technique, we stabilized the light to a fractional stability 6×10^{-19} at 100 seconds. (c) 2008 Google - Map data (c) 2008 Tele Atlas.

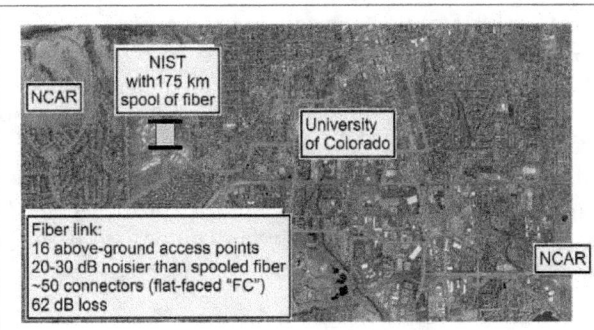

Contact

Nathan Newbury

(301) 497-4227

nathan.newbury@nist.gov

QUANTUM INFORMATION
AND TERAHERTZ TECHNOLOGY

Summary

Our nation requires the flow of information for the banking industry, the military, and others to be completely secure. Coding information with single particles of light (photons) holds the key to ultimate protection from eavesdropping, guaranteed by the laws of physics. This project develops devices and measurements that enable world-record-setting demonstrations of secure communications. Sensors that can detect concealed weapons and explosives under clothing are critical to homeland security. Terahertz imaging systems are capable of revealing objects and chemicals that metal detectors cannot, but without the risk that X-rays pose. This project develops the terahertz systems and measurements that enable applications including airport security, aircraft navigation, and industrial processing.

Description

This project has two main focuses – the development of optical photon technologies for quantum information science and technology and the development and application of terahertz and millimeter-wave technology and metrology for imaging and spectroscopy.

In the development of single photonics for quantum information science and technology, researchers work closely with the Nanostructure Fabrication and Metrology Project on the generation of novel non-classical states of light and the detection of single photons. Currently, EEEL investigates the use of nonlinear fibers and nonlinear crystals as a source of correlated photon pairs or squeezed light and is manipulating the squeezed light to make Schroedinger "Cat" states of light. In addition to making non-classical states of light, EEEL researchers build detector systems that are the best in the world at operating at the single photon level. Presently, this project is primarily focused on using two different superconducting detector technologies – transition-edge sensors (TES) and superconducting nanowire single-photon detectors (SNSPD).

Over the past several years, the "Terahertz" portion of this project has focused on bolometric detection of THz radiation. Initial work on cryogenic detectors has been extended to antenna-coupled bolometers operating at room temperature. These detectors provide a rugged, low-cost alternative for homeland security applications; e.g., mobile police units or portal scanners in airports. Researchers have established that imaging in the terahertz frequency range has the potential for effectively detecting weapons and contraband concealed by clothing. EEEL staff members have fabricated a focal plane array of antenna-coupled bolometers and demonstrated best-in-class, real-time imaging. Plans are to continue to explore applications of room-temperature (uncooled) and cryogenic antenna-coupled micro-bolometers and perform side-by-side imaging of the same scenes with passive and actively illuminated terahertz camera systems to help settle many outstanding pheno-menological questions, such as the capability of terahertz systems to selectively identify specific target materials.

Major Accomplishments

- Demonstrated the highest system detection efficiency for single photons, >95 % at 1550 nm.
- Demonstrated, for the first time, time-correlated single-photon counting with superconducting single-photon detectors.
- Developed and demonstrated an ultra-wideband, millimeter-wave/terahertz detector array for use in contraband detection (with VTT of Finland).
- Developed and characterized a novel, aqueous blackbody calibration (ABC) source for calibrating optical power in the mm-wave to terahertz frequency band.

Selected Publications

- D. Petrovykh, H. Kimura-Suda, A. Opdahl, L. Richter, M. J. Tarlov, L. Whitman, "Alkanethiols on Platinum: Multicomponent Self-Assembled Monolayers," Langmuir, Vol. 22, No. 6 (2006)
- D. Petrovykh, V. Perez-Dieste, A. Opdahl, H. Kimura-Suda, J. Sullivan, M. J. Tarlov, F. Himpsel, L. Whitman, "Nucleobase Orientation and Ordering in Films of Single-Stranded DNA on Gold," Journal of the American Chemical Society, Vol. 128, No. 1 (2006)
- K. Balss, C. T. Avedisian, R. Cavicchi, M. J. Tarlov, "Nanosecond Imaging of Microboiling Behavior on Pulsed-Heated Au Films Modified With Hydrophilic and Hydrophobic Self-Assembled Monolayers," Langmuir, Vol. 21, No. 23 (2005)

Figure 2. Four tungsten transition-edge sensors with aluminum wiring. The upper two are 25 μm by 25 μm. The lower two sensors are 50 μm by 50 μm.

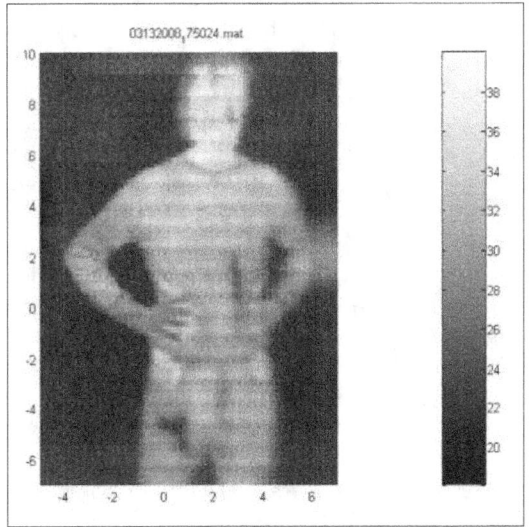

Figure 1. Passive millimeter-wave image of concealed contraband (handgun and ceramic knife).

Contact

Sae Woo Nam

(303) 497-3148

saewoo.nam@nist.gov

NANOSTRUCTURE
FABRICATION AND METROLOGY

Summary

The photon is the fundamental particle of light, analogous to the electron as the fundamental carrier of electric charge. Project members generate, manipulate, and detect single photons, which require making nanoscale structures a few tens of atoms wide or less. Confined in this manner, the photons and electrons exhibit "quantum" properties much different from those physical properties exhibited by larger objects. In particular, the uncertainty associated with large numbers of particles can be eliminated, and measurement accuracy to the fundamental limit can be achieved. The single-photon emitters and true photon counters developed at NIST enable its scientists to produce and characterize new quantum states of light that will push measurement science far beyond its current limits over the next decade.

Description

This project develops semiconductor nanostructures, especially self-assembled quantum dots and photonic crystals, for a variety of applications including single photonics, laser diodes, and quantum optical metrology. It also develops quantum optical metrology based on other sources and detectors (not based on semiconductor nanostructures). It collaborates extensively with the Quantum Information and Terahertz Technology Project and with JILA to accomplish some of its goals.

Semiconductor quantum dot sources of single photons and entangled photon pairs offer many advantages compared to competing quantum emitter sources. The quantum dots can be tailored to emit at specific wavelengths. The spontaneous emission lifetime is 1 ns, which leads to very high rates of single-photon emission. Perhaps the biggest advantage of these sources is that they are easily integrated with high-finesse cavities, enabling even faster emission and directional output. High-speed and high-efficiency single-photon sources are an important enabler of quantum communications and the traceability of optical power to the photon.

Quantum-dot-based detectors of single photons exhibit linear gain at ultralow photon fluxes, which enables them to count the number of photons in a pulse of light. The photon number-resolving capability of the detector developed by the Nanostructure Fabrication and Metrology Project is unique in compound-semiconductor-based devices.

Quantum dot lasers were initially investigated because they were expected to have low threshold currents, have high differential gain and modulation bandwidths, and be temperature-insensitive. Although not all of these predictions have been realized, quantum dot lasers have demonstrated some previously unpredicted and unusual behavior. This project, in collaboration with JILA, has recently demonstrated wavelength bistability in a two-section monolithic quantum dot laser and also a "dark pulse" laser, a novel pulsed laser in which the pulses have lower intensity than the DC level.

Major Accomplishments

- Developed a photon-number resolving detector based on quantum dots (Quantum Dot Optically Gated Field Effect Transistor, QDOGFET).
- Demonstrated a type of mode-locked laser that produces "dark pulses."
- Demonstrated a bistable, switchable quantum dot laser.
- Developed spectral-hole-burning technique to demonstrate that exciton coherence time in a quantum dot is limited only by the spontaneous emission lifetime.
- Measured $g^{(3)}$ and $g^{(4)}$, the third- and fourth-order intensity correlation, from a pseudothermal source of light.

Selected Publications

- E. J. Gansen, M. A. Rowe, M. B. Greene, D. Rosenberg, T. E. Harvey, M. Y. Su, R. H. Hadfield, S. W. Nam, R. P. Mirin, "Photon-Number-Discriminating Detection Using a Quantum-Dot, Optically Gated, Field-effect Transistor," Nature Photonics 1, 585 (2007)
- M. Feng, N. A. Brilliant, S. T. Cundiff, R. P. Mirin, K. L. Silverman, "Wavelength Bistability in Two-Section Mode-Locked Quantum-Dot Diode Lasers," IEEE Phot. Tech. Lett. 19, 804 (2007)
- J. J. Berry, M. J. Stevens, R. P. Mirin, K. L. Silverman, "High-Resolution Spectral Hole Burning in $In_xGa_{1-x}As/GaAs$ Quantum Dots," Appl. Phys. Lett. 88, 061114 (2006)

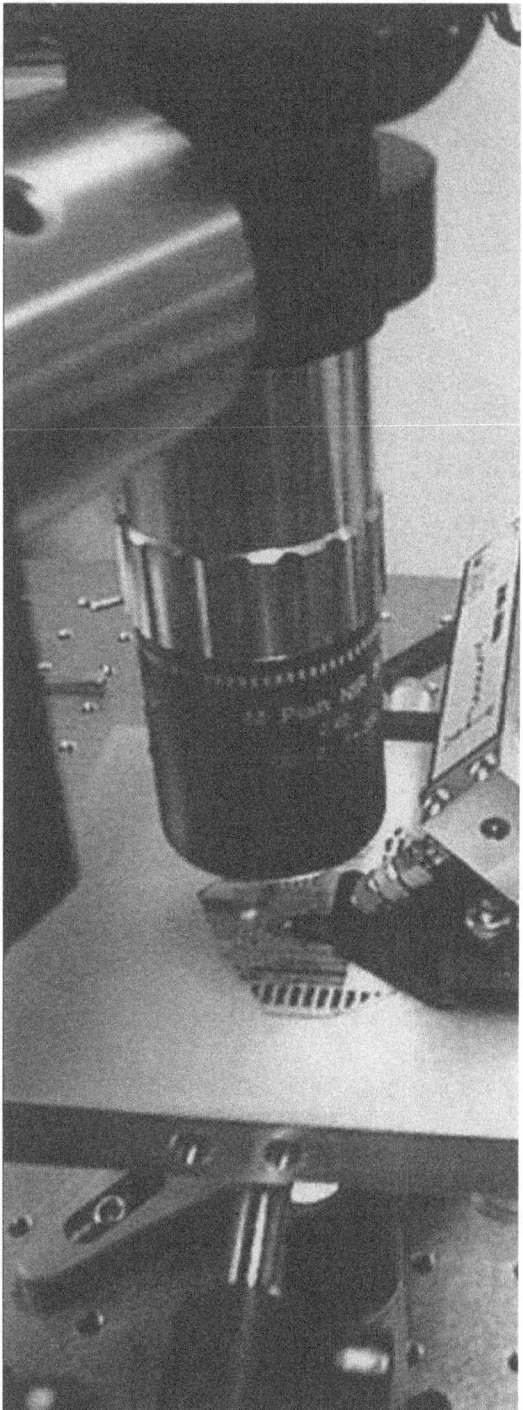

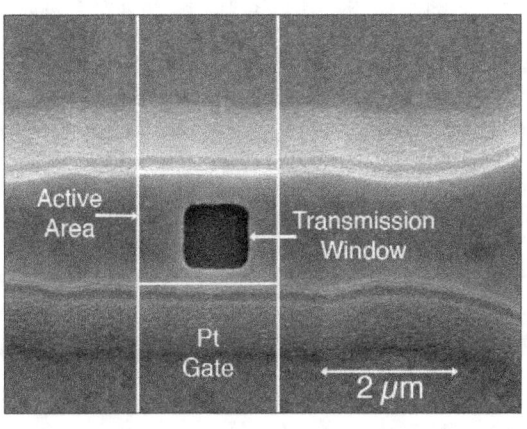

Figure 1. A scanning electron micrograph of a QDOGFET device used for photon-number resolving detection.

Contact

Richard Mirin

(303) 497-7955

richard.mirin@nist.gov

SEMICONDUCTOR GROWTH
AND DEVICES

Summary

At the heart of a DVD player, or in the fiber optic system that transmits telephone calls and data, lies a tiny crystal of semiconductor that emits laser light. That semiconductor chip has been produced, or "grown," in a sophisticated piece of equipment to make it pure and efficient for light generation and detection. This project advances cutting-edge research in improving semiconductor crystal growth for devices that generate, control, and sense light. One emphasis is on precisely growing nanowires one-thousand times narrower than a human hair. These structures hold promise for enabling high-efficiency solar energy cells and energy-saving lighting to combat our nation's dependence on fossil fuel, as well as microscopic sensors and lasers for the early detection and treatment of cancer.

Description

Compound semiconductor materials form the basis for the diode lasers, LEDs, photodetectors, and high-efficiency solar cells critical to optical communication, display, data storage, and energy conservation and generation. Many of these semiconductor devices now incorporate structures with a high degree of strain and nanostructures so small that the properties of the devices depend on their physical dimensions as well as the bulk materials properties.

A major focus in this project is the growth and processing of GaN nanowires for nanometrology and device applications. Staff in the project have grown GaN nanowires with catalyst-free molecular beam epitaxy (MBE) that are strain-free, very low in chemical impurities, and usually entirely free of structural defects. These properties lead to high optical emission intensity, consistent doping behavior, and high mechanical resonance quality factors, all of which are needed for future technical applications that will surpass GaN thin films in performance. The nanowire architecture is also a framework for inventing new characterization tools and devices. A simple example is that the optical emission can be used to measure externally applied strain. Future devices will extend this work on nanowires-as-transistors and light emitters to include nanowire lasers, biosensor applications, near-field optical probes, oscillators for communications equipment, single-photon emitters and detectors, and integration of photonics with silicon circuitry.

The scientific understanding needed to engineer these devices will make use of this project's basic research in quantum dot and nanowire nucleation and growth mechanisms, including the role of strain in nanostructures. This project supports manufacturing of compound semiconductor devices with the world's only composition standards for these materials. EEEL staff also lead a cavity ringdown spectroscopy program that focuses on direct measurement of impurities in the source gases used in compound semiconductor manufacturing. Researchers have achieved sensitivity below 50 nmol mol^{-1} for water in arsine and below 10 nmol mol^{-1} for water in phosphine.

Major Accomplishments

- Grew and characterized defect-free GaN nanowires, leading to an R&D Micro Nano 25 Award for NIST in 2006.
- Developed a comprehensive model for estimating carrier concentration and mobility based on nanowire resistance.
- Explained the role of growth parameters in the uniformity of InGaAs quantum dot size and spacing.
- Applied, for the first time, cavity ringdown spectroscopy to measure water vapor as a contaminant in arsine and phosphine.
- Released AlGaAs composition Standard Reference Materials in 2006.

Selected Publications

- L. M. Mansfield, K. A. Bertness, P. T. Blanchard, T. E. Harvey, A. W. Sanders, N. A. Sanford, "GaN Nanowire Carrier Concentration Calculated from Light and Dark Resistance Measurements," submitted to the Journal of Electronic Materials (2008)
- K. A. Bertness, A. Roshko, L. M. Mansfield, T. E. Harvey, N. A. Sanford, "Mechanism for Spontaneous Growth of GaN Nanowires with Molecular Beam Epitaxy," Journal of Crystal Growth, Vol. 310, 3154-3158 (2008)
- S. M. Tanner, J. M. Gray, C. T. Rogers, K. A. Bertness, N. A. Sanford, "High-Q GaN Nanowire Resonators and Oscillators," Applied Physics Letters, Vol. 91, 203117 (2007)

Figure 1. Scanning electron microscopy picture of GaN nanowires grown with catalyst-free MBE, with insert showing nanowire tips. Note the hexagonal cross-section, consistent high aspect ratio, and flexibility of nanowires.

Contact

Kris Bertness

(303) 497-5069

kristine.bertness@nist.gov

OPTICAL MATERIALS
METROLOGY

Summary

The 21st century has heightened needs for conserving energy, producing clean energy at low cost, and providing safety and security at home and abroad. To fully optimize energy-efficient lighting and displays, next-generation solar cells, and sensors, NIST scientists are measuring the critical properties of optical materials. Especially important are nano-engineered structures for new technologies, since the fundamental properties of nanostructures are not the same as those for bulk materials. This project has made remarkable advances in developing measurement tools and methods for optical materials that enable enhanced products. A particular focus is on semiconductor nanowires, a breakthrough technology offering superior capabilities for future-generation microscopes, lighting, photovoltaics, cell phones, and other electronics.

Description

It is internationally recognized that LED-based solid-state lighting using III-nitride semiconductors (GaN, AlGaN, InGaN) is poised to significantly reduce energy demand for the 21st century. Illumination consumes approximately 30 % of the U.S. energy budget. Due to various complications, conventional planar LEDs made from these materials are inherently inefficient. Moreover, the planar morphology also results in low-light extraction efficiency. There is much room for improving LEDs in order to meet the looming worldwide demands on reduced lighting costs in the face of mounting energy costs.

NIST scientists found that the GaN is fundamentally superior when grown as nanowires instead of planar films. They also quickly realized that dense nanowire arrays would enable LEDs with greatly improved light extraction efficiency. These findings, conclusions, and motivations aimed at developing nanowires for LED illumination technology have been arrived at independently by competing research groups around the world. EEEL is in a strong position since EEEL-grown nanowires are proven to be some of the best in the world, and NIST has developed new metrology methods to analyze these nanostructures. EEEL staff can also grow nanowires on silicon substrates, thus enabling numerous possibilities in new device integration. Recently, project staff teamed with a DARPA sponsored "iMINT" University Focus Center on nanotechnology. Of 11 such Centers now sponsored by the DARPA MTO office, DARPA has publicly recognized NIST's progress in GaN nanowires as one of the 3 most significant outcomes of all 11 Centers. The dense nanowire morphology also enables improved light collection efficiency. Recent advances include starting work to use nanowires for improving photovoltaic devices as well.

Nanowire LEDs and lasers are also developed for new active-tip near-field scanning optical microscopy (NSOM) tools for metrology. Additionally, EEEL researchers are working on the application of nanowires for cancer research and advanced sensors for biological and chemical agents.

Major Accomplishments

- Demonstrated the first core-sleeve nanowire heterostructures employing MBE-grown Si-doped cores and HVPE-grown Mg-doped sleeves.
- Demonstrated the best measurement to date for the surface recombination velocity of GaN.
- Demonstrated the best GaN nanowire Metal-Semiconductor Field Effect Transistor (MESFET) devices to date.
- Demonstrated the use of steady state and transient photoconductivity to estimate carrier concentration, mobility, and capture cross section for nanowires.
- Demonstrated nanowire UV detectors sensitive to only a few hundred photons per second.

Selected Publications

- B. Schlager, K. A. Bertness, P. T. Blanchard, L. H. Robins, A. Roshko, N. A. Sanford, "Steady-State and Time-Resolved Photoluminescence from Relaxed and Strained GaN Nanowires Grown by Catalyst-Free Molecular-Beam Epitaxy," Journal of Applied Physics 103, 124309 (2008)
- P. T. Blanchard, K. A. Bertness, T. E. Harvey, L. M. Mansfield, A. W. Sanders, N. A. Sanford, "Metal-Semiconductor Field Effect Transistors (MESFETs) Made from Individual GaN Nanowires," IEEE Transactions on Nanotechnology (to be published, 2008)
- S. M. Tanner, J. M. Gray, C. T. Rogers, K. A. Bertness, N. A. Sanford, "High-Q GaN Nanowire Resonators and Oscillators," Applied Physics Letters 91, 203117 (2007)

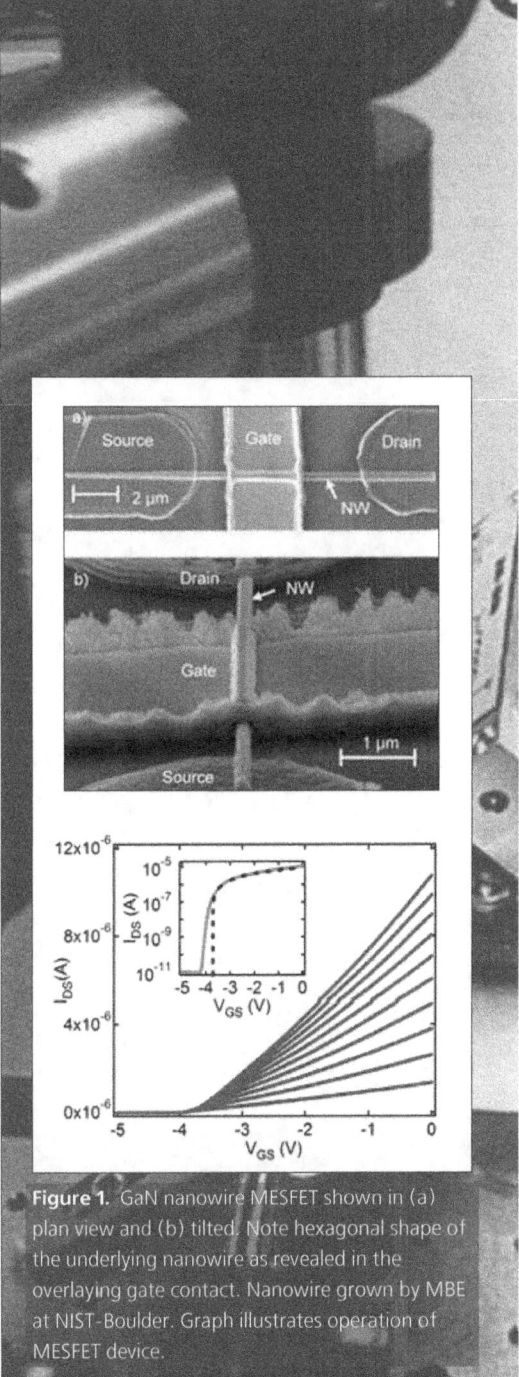

Figure 1. GaN nanowire MESFET shown in (a) plan view and (b) tilted. Note hexagonal shape of the underlying nanowire as revealed in the overlaying gate contact. Nanowire grown by MBE at NIST-Boulder. Graph illustrates operation of MESFET device.

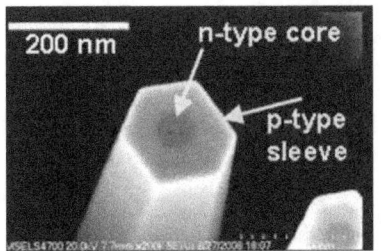

Figure 2. Core-sleeve p-n GaN nanowire heterostructure. n-type Si-doped core and p-type Mg-doped sleeve are indicated. Core grown by MBE at NIST-Boulder, sleeve subsequently overgrown by HVPE at NIST-Gaithersburg.

Contact

Norman A. Sanford

(303) 497-5239

norman.sanford@nist.gov

QUANTUM ELECTRICAL METROLOGY
DIVISION

The Quantum Electrical Metrology Division unites fundamental electrical metrology and leading-edge quantum-based measurement research to create a dynamic organization with a mission to lead quantum electrical metrology into the future. The division consists of three groups: Fundamental Electrical Measurements, Applied Electrical Metrology, and Quantum Devices. The first two groups are located in Gaithersburg, MD, and boast of a proud 100-year history of precision electrical metrology. The Quantum Devices Group located in Boulder, CO, brings a 35-year history of creating world-leading quantum-based standards and measurement systems. The division works to provide the world's best electrically based measurements and standards.

The project descriptions that follow give a detailed description of the work underway in the division. The research falls into three general categories. The division has the responsibility to realize and advance our understanding of the fundamental electrical "units," including the volt (both DC and AC), the ohm, and the farad. This work also extends to measuring fundamental constants, with world-leading work on measuring Planck's constant through electrical measurements using a Watt balance and new work measuring Boltzmann's constant through electrical (Johnson) noise. The division also provides U.S. industry and other National Metrology Institutes (NMIs) with connection to the electrical units through calibration services and measurement expertise. This includes interlaboratory comparisons and more recently the creation and dissemination of quantum-based electrical standards that allow the highest level of measurement precision to be achieved outside of NIST. Finally, the division uses its expertise in electrical measurements and quantum effects to develop new measurement methods and systems that extend our capabilities into new regimes, such as quantum voltage systems, quantum computing and quantum limited measurements, and quantum sensors for electromagnetic radiation from microwaves through gamma rays.

The division has a staff of about 120, which includes government employees as well as guest researchers, post-doctoral associates, contractors, and graduate and undergraduate students. With facilities on both the Gaithersburg and Boulder campuses, the division has far-reaching ties with universities, government agencies, other NMIs, and U.S. industry. The division's outreach, which also includes visiting industrial and other sites, attending and sponsoring conferences, and hosting numerous visitors at both campuses, greatly increases the impact and dissemination of our work.

QUANTUM VOLTAGE SYSTEM DEVELOPMENT AND DISSEMINATION

Summary

Accurate representation of the volt and precise techniques for measuring voltage are essential to the electrical and electronics industries. Determining how to do this throughout the U.S. with extraordinary accuracy is one of the main roles of EEEL.
This is accomplished by developing new quantum standards using Josephson junctions, superconductor-based devices whose quantum behavior makes them perfect frequency-to-voltage converters. EEEL scientists are using this property to create extremely accurate DC and AC voltage standards and also to develop novel methods for the precise measurement of other fundamental electrical quantities.

Description

In 1990, an international agreement redefined the volt in terms of the voltage generated by a superconducting integrated circuit developed jointly at NIST and the Physikalisch-Technische Bundesanstalt (PTB), Germany's NMI. The circuit contains thousands of Josephson junctions, each one a sandwich consisting of an insulating layer between two superconducting segments and having a typical thickness of a few hundred nanometers.

Current will flow across a Josephson junction despite the insulating layer, and, with alternating current (ac), a voltage develops across the junction that is exactly proportional to the ac frequency. This relationship depends only on fundamental constants of quantum physics and does not depend on the physical properties of the junction, such as its dimensions or environmental conditions like temperature. Josephson junctions, as perfect frequency-to-voltage converters, provide a quantum basis for a voltage standard because frequencies can be defined with enormous precision.

Josephson voltage standard systems have been deployed around the world since 1990, greatly improving the uniformity of voltage measurements. One key development at NIST is the programmable Josephson voltage standard (PJVS) system, which can provide desired voltages with an uncertainty better than a few parts in a billion. PJVS replicas are used at NIST and throughout the world to provide voltage calibrations for a variety of applications, particularly experiments that measure other electrical units. The system is regularly used in the NIST voltage calibration lab and is also being implemented in a novel electric power calibration system that will provide the electric power industry with the world's most precise electrical standards, which, in turn, support the reliable operation of the electrical power grid.

Project scientists have also made substantial improvements to the process of accurately transferring a fundamental standard to end users. For example, we have developed a portable, compact Josephson voltage standard (CJVS) that scientists can carry with them to compare Josephson voltage systems in different geographic locations. The CJVS decreased end-user uncertainty by a factor of 10 or better.

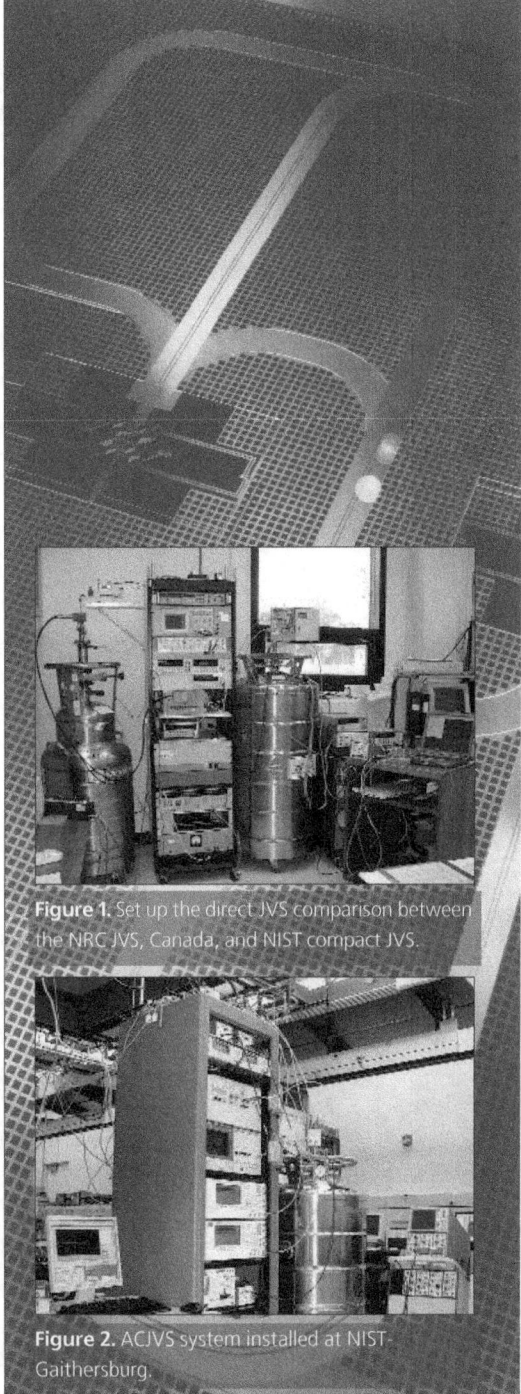

Major Accomplishments

- Developed an ac Josephson voltage standard (ACJVS) that provides the most accurate ac voltage measurements ever made.
- Developed a protocol to successfully compare the NIST Compact Josephson Voltage Standard (CJVS) with the JVS of National Research Council (NRC) Canada.
- Performed a direct JVS comparison with Lockheed Martin Mission Services in Denver and found a difference between the two systems of a few parts in 10^{10}, a result that supports traceability of SI units for U.S. industry and other government agencies.

Selected Publications

- Y. Tang, "Application of NIST Compact Josephson Voltage Standard for Intercomparison," Proceedings of International Conference on Advances in Metrology 2006, Dec.11 -16, 2006, New Delhi, India (2006)
- S. K. Jaiswal, J. Sims, and Y. Tang, "Characterization of a Low Thermal Scanner for Automatic Voltage Measurement with the NIST Josephson Voltage Standard," Measurement Science Conference Proceedings, January 22 - 26, 2007, Long Beach, CA (2007)
- T. E. Lipe, J. R. Kinard, Y. Tang and J. E. Sims, "Improvements in the NIST Calibration Service for Thermal Transfer Standards," NCSLI MEASURE, Vol. 2, No. 1, pp. 70-74 (2007)

Figure 3. NIST provided a link for Centro Nacional de Metrología (CENAM) to Bureau International des Poids et Measures (BIPM) via a JVS comparison (notice that the pink point representing the CENAM measurement has one of the best links to BIPM).

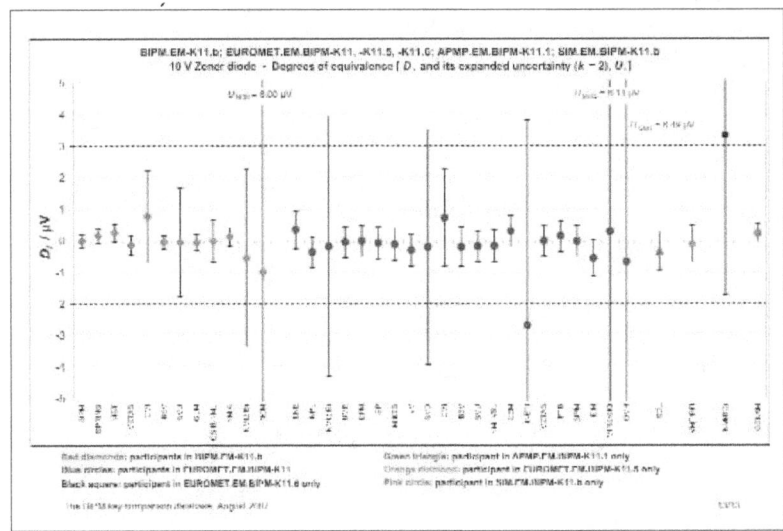

Contact

Thomas Lipe

(301) 975-4251

thomas.lipe@nist.gov

METROLOGY OF THE OHM

Summary

Resistance standards traceable to NIST provide references for measurements of current at levels from 2000 A to below 1 pA and are used to support a wide variety of impedance, temperature, strain, and power measurements. This project develops the technology of quantum electrical measurements including the world's best high-resistance standards and superconducting quantum interference device (SQUID)-based scaling techniques. EEEL maintains close working relationships with researchers in other leading NMIs and successfully completed 2 bilateral comparisons with the Bureau International des Poids et Measures (BIPM) and piloted 5 international key comparisons in the past 10 years. This leadership has resulted in collaborative research to develop and deploy sophisticated multi-function, high-precision, and low-maintenance cryogenic current comparators (CCCs) of a new NIST design, which have been installed and tested at NIST and are being installed at NMIs in Argentina, Australia, and Mexico.

Description

The Ohm Project has been a leader in providing internationally consistent resistance standards that are readily available to support the scientific and industrial foundations of the U.S. economy. Through this very broad customer base, the activities of the project enable cost-effective electrical measurements at NIST and at more than 300 U.S. sites, leading to improved performance of products and services in a competitive world environment. The resistance calibration service brings a yearly income to NIST of several hundred thousands of dollars as well as supporting over a dozen other calibration areas. Project staff members provide extensive customer contact and consultation on topics including teraohmmeter measurements, the characterization processes used with resistive shunts at very high current levels, and power loading measurements to support a recent Air Force contract. Project scientists work in the U.S. and international communities, including support for comparisons at low, moderate, and high resistance levels and development of improved standards and techniques for better agreement between primary references.

The project collaborates in research on nanometer scale single-electron devices designed as biometric sensors, and two members participate in the new Quantum Conductance Project that aims to develop quantum Hall resistance (QHR) devices from graphene. Project staff members pursue scientific breakthroughs to maintain accurate local representations of the unit (conventional standards) and to develop improved quantum metrology, including the recent introduction of resistive-winding cryogenic current comparators (CCCs) that enable stable SQUID operation with improved current sensitivity. This advance was combined with a two-terminal CCC bridge design that NIST developed in the 1970s, and provides the world's only direct CCC scaling from the QHR to resistance values from 100 k to 100 M and above.

Major Accomplishments

- Piloted SIM Key Comparisons at 1 Ω, 1 MΩ, and 1 GΩ; developed analysis to link Systema Interamericano de Metrología (SIM) NMIs to the international community.
- Automated and reported 1000 V dual-calibrator bridge measurements using fully guarded robotic actuators.
- Developed CCCs for scaling up to 1 GΩ with multiple links to the QHR standard; disseminating the measurement techniques to three other NMIs.
- At CPEM08, presented CCC work, SIM results, and teraohmmeter automation. Collaborated on two papers presented by other NMIs.
- At NCSLI-2008, presented papers on power loading in 1 Ω resistors and teraohmmeter procedures.

Selected Publications

- R. E. Elmquist, D. G. Jarrett, N. F. Zhang, "SIM RMO Comparison Report; 1 Ω, 1 MΩ, and 1 GΩ," submitted to BIPM, to be published in Metrologia Tech. Supp. (2008)
- G. R. Jones and R. E. Elmquist, "Power Loading Effects in Precision 1 Ω Resistors," NCSLI Conf. Proc., August 3-7, 2008. Extended version accepted for NCSLI Measure (2008)
- D. G. Jarrett, M. E. Kraft, I. Castro, B. Degler, M. Evans "Procedures for the Traceability of High-Resistance Standards Using a Teraohmmeter," NCSLI Conf. Proc., August 3-7, 2008. Extended version accepted for NCSLI Measure (2008)

Figure 1. Guest Researcher Marcos Bierzychudek (INTI, Argentina) with R. Elmquist and M. Kraft setting up a CCC cryostat in the AML Resistance lab.

Figure 2. Guest Researcher Dr. F. Hernandez (CENAM, Mexico) tests one of four high-resistance CCC systems constructed in 2008.

Figure 3. Summer Undergraduate Research Fellowship researcher A. Mercado helps develop a characterization process for insulating materials to be used in a NASA probe.

Contact

Rand Elmquist

(301) 975-6591

elmquist@nist.gov

QUANTUM CONDUCTANCE/ GRAPHENE-BASED QUANTUM METROLOGY

Summary

Graphene is a new material with truly extraordinary electronic properties that has great potential in many areas where conventional materials are running into obstacles. Although conceptually graphene is an unrolled carbon nanotube (CNT), graphene transcends the limitations of CNTs by offering the potential to fabricate complete systems entirely out of graphene, ranging from the macro to nanoscale. The opportunities for both exciting new science and important applications have led to an explosion of research on graphene at universities, domestic and foreign national labs, and industrial labs.

The goal of the Quantum Conductance Project is to develop graphene metrology for intrinsic electrical standards, specifically near-room-temperature quantum Hall resistance standards.

Description

Progress in fundamental electrical standards and electronics is usually incremental and based on brute force engineering with sporadic episodes of ingenuity. Graphene represents one of these rare opportunities to dramatically improve measurement capabilities by utilizing a completely new scientific principle. However, application of the truly unique characteristics of graphene requires measuring the physical properties and developing new fabrication methods. EEEL's efforts are currently focused on developing graphene to advance NIST's core mission — specifically, the development of intrinsic quantum electrical standards and metrology to enable the development of innovative future electronics.

Since the first quantum Hall resistance (QHR) standards were developed over 25 years ago, fabrication of improved GaAs-GaAlAs heterostructures has been a goal of leading National Metrology Institutes (NMIs) around the world; however, they are consistently in short supply because of the difficulty in producing even moderate quality QHR standards. Operating today's QHR devices requires extensive cryogenic equipment and expertise; thus NMIs currently disseminate resistance through artifact standards. These have limited accuracy and are inherently unstable, resulting in time consuming and costly calibrations. New graphene-based QHR standards with higher-temperature operation have the promise to greatly improve the dissemination of quantum-based resistance metrology to customers.

In microelectronics, it is well known that the continuation of Moore's Law is already facing major challenges in power management and is being confronted by the discreteness of matter itself. The U.S. semiconductor industry spends billions of dollars to make incremental advances and desperately needs technology that transcends CMOS limitations. The major semiconductor industries have established consortia such as the Nanoelectronics Research Initiative (NRI) to direct various laboratories (academic, national, and corporate) to come up with visionary solutions to the foreshadowed limitations in silicon. Graphene promises to be one of these potential solutions, and we will exploit the new opportunities for discovery offered by graphene that specifically apply to electrical metrology.

Major Accomplishments

- Organized collaborative research program on graphene with other NIST Laboratories and leading U.S. research groups.
- Fabricated exfoliated graphene on Si/SiO_2 substrate for testing.
- Fabricated first graphene devices at NIST in the Center for Nanoscale Science and Technology (CNST).
- Measured external collaborator's graphene quantum resistance standard against national resistance standards to 3 %.

Selected Publications

- D. Petrovykh, H. Kimura-Suda, A. Opdahl, L. Richter, M. J. Tarlov, L. Whitman, "Alkanethiols on Platinum: Multicomponent Self-Assembled Monolayers," Langmuir, Vol. 22, No. No. 6, (2006)
- D. Petrovykh, V. Perez-Dieste, A. Opdahl, H. Kimura-Suda, J. Sullivan, M. J. Tarlov, F. Himpsel, L. Whitman, "Nucleobase Orientation and Ordering in Films of Single-Stranded DNA on Gold," Journal of the American Chemical Society, Vol. 128, No. 1, (2006)
- K. Balss, C. T. Avedisian, R. Cavicchi, M. J. Tarlov, "Nanosecond Imaging of Microboiling Behavior on Pulsed-Heated Au Films Modified With Hydrophilic and Hydrophobic Self-Assembled Monolayers," Langmuir, Vol. 21, No. No. 23, (2005)

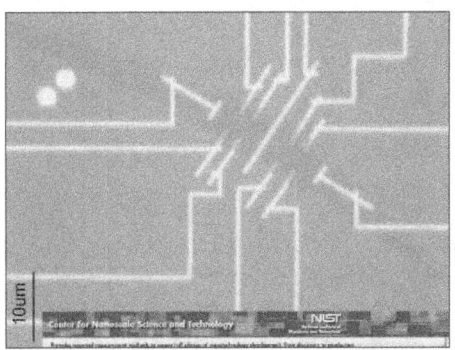

Figure 1. Graphene Hall bar developed at NIST by undergraduate students.

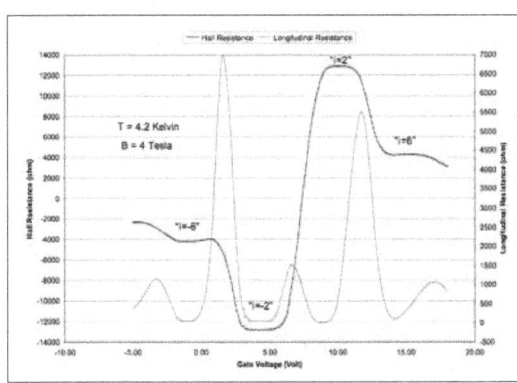

Figure 2. Graphene Hall plateaus measured with respect to national standards.

Contact

David Newell

(301) 975-4228

david.newell@nist.gov

AC-DC DIFFERENCE

Summary

Extremely accurate measurements of an unchanging voltage signal can be made relatively routinely using a quantum voltage source. However, for many real-life applications, the accurate measurement of a varying electrical signal is a more important and challenging measurement need. The NIST AC-DC Difference Project provides U.S. industry with the essential link between ac and the corresponding DC electrical standards via a world-class calibration service, and, through cutting-edge research into new AC-DC difference measurement techniques, employs both quantum standards and standards fabricated in novel ways.

Description

The use of thermal converters for ac voltage metrology was introduced by Frank Hermach at NIST in 1952. The basic thermal converter is a thermo-element, consisting of a thermocouple positioned at the midpoint of a heater wire, enclosed in an evacuated bulb. The thermoelement senses the heat generated by an electrical signal applied to the heater. By comparing the heating effect of an unknown AC signal to that of the average of both polarities of a known DC signal, the Root Mean Square (RMS) AC quantity may be measured in terms of the known DC quantity, giving the AC-DC difference of the thermal converter. The traditional thermoelement has an input voltage of a few volts or an input current of a few milliamperes, with a best uncertainty of about 1 µV/V or µA/A over the frequency range from 10 Hz to 1 MHz. In combination with a precision resistor or shunt, the thermal converter is commonly used at voltages up to 1000 V and currents up to 100 A and, in combination with amplifier circuits, is used at voltages as low as 2 mV.

The fundamental errors in thermo-elements are thermoelectric errors, produced when a current flows through a temperature gradient. These thermo-electric errors may be reduced by adding more thermocouples and using the thermoelement at a reduced input amplitude. The resulting device, the Multijunction Thermal Converter (MJTC), is the most accurate means of measuring AC voltage and current at voltages above 500 mV and currents up to 50 mA; uncertainties of about 5×10^{-7} or less are possible in the audio frequency. Unfortunately, traditional MJTCs made with wire are difficult to make and nearly impossible to obtain.

To address this problem, NIST is presently making MJTCs using semiconductor fabrication techniques. These devices fall into two broad categories; one type of MJTCs is designed for high-frequency AC voltage metrology, the other for high-current AC metrology. The high-frequency MJTCs (Fig. 1) are fabricated on quartz substrates, for reduced dielectric loss, and are predicted to have very small AC-DC differences up to 100 MHz at a few volts. The high-current MJTCs (Fig. 2) have very large heater structures capable of taking currents up to 1 A. We plan to parallel up to eight of these high-current MJTCs in a single module to achieve a 10 A current converter. Initial results are very encouraging, and we anticipate using both of these MJTCs in our measurement services before the end of the year.

In addition to new artifact standards, in collaboration with the Quantum Voltage Project, we are developing a quantum standard for AC voltage, based on pulse-programmable Josephson Junctions. We have already provided a quantum-based calibration to a customer with reductions in uncertainty of as much as 98 % over uncertainties obtained using traditional scaling techniques. The AC Josephson Voltage Standard (ACJVS, Fig. 3) promises unprecedented reductions in uncertainty over its operating range of 2 mV to about 275 mV and, coupled with MJTCs, should allow us to substantially reduce the uncertainties for AC voltage metrology.

Major Accomplishments

- Fabricated prototype multijunction thermal converters based on quartz substrates for AC voltage measurements up to 100 MHz.
- Fabricated prototype multijunction thermal converters based on silicon substrates for AC current measurements up to 1 A.
- Began dissemination of AC voltage based on ACJVS, providing the most accurate calibrations of AC-DC difference ever made.
- Reduced current converter uncertainties at 100 A and 100 kHz from about 1200 µA/A to about 200 µA/A using NIST-built two-stage current transformers and shunts.

Selected Publications

- T. E. Lipe, J. R. Kinard, Y. Tang, S. P. Benz, C. J. Burroughs, P. D. Dresselhaus, "Thermal Voltage Converter Calibrations using a Quantum AC Source," Metrologia, vol. 45, pp. 275-280 (2008)
- P. S. Filipski, J. R. Kinard, T. E. Lipe, Y. Tang, S. P. Benz, "Correction of Systematic Errors Due to the Voltage Leads in AC Josephson Voltage Standard," in CPEM 2008 Digest, pp. 598-599, CPEM 2008, Broomfield, CO (2008)
- L. Scarioni, T. E. Lipe, J. R. Kinard, "Design and Fabrication of MJTCs on Quartz Substrates at NIST," in CPEM 2008 Digest, pp. 648-649, CPEM 2008, Broomfield, CO (2008)

Figure 1. Photograph of quartz-based multijunction thermal converter.

Figure 2. Photograph of 1 A MJTC current converter.

Figure 3.
ACJVS system installed at NIST-Gaithersburg.

Contact

Thomas E. Lipe

(301) 975-4251

thomas.lipe@nist.gov

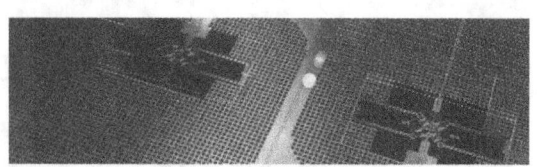

FARAD AND IMPEDANCE
METROLOGY

Summary

Accurate capacitance measurements are essential for electronic systems and sensors. This project aims to provide the world's best basis for accurate impedance measurements by tying the U.S. legal system of electrical units to the International System of Units (SI) through the realization of the SI unit of capacitance. This work also forms the foundation of NIST's measurement services for electrical impedance, ensuring a sound metrological basis for impedance measurements, both nationally and internationally, and ensuring that the claims of measurement accuracy by U.S. industries are recognized and accepted worldwide.

The need continues for a better representation of capacitance and also for better calibration tools at NIST with which researchers can objectively verify claims of improved performance specifications, to achieve consistency and help avoid technical trade barriers.

Description

The primary facility for connecting the U.S. legal system of electrical units to the international system of units is the NIST calculable capacitor, with which the measurement of capacitance is effectively achieved through a measurement of length. Both the calculable capacitor and the chain of high-precision measurements that transfers the SI unit to the calibration laboratories is maintained, improved, and compared with other National Metrology Institutes to ensure measurement consistency on an international level.

Over the last few decades, NIST has successfully invested in two key quantum representations of electrical quantities; both the Quantum Hall Resistance (QHR) and Josephson Voltage standards have now achieved measurement uncertainties approaching parts in 10^9. These quantum standards, however, represent only a few points in a multi-dimensional world of electrical measurements. The crucial link between the fundamental electrical standards and commercial electronic instrumentation is provided by precision ac measurement standards. A combination of transformer techniques and modern Digital Signal Processor (DSP) techniques has the potential to extend our expertise over a much wider dynamic range.

Consistency between resistance and impedance measurement services from NIST is expected by the instrumentation industry and DOD laboratories. An improved resistance-capacitance (RC) link is also needed to realize the farad from the QHR standard, if the proposed redefinition of the SI occurs in the near future, and to advance basic research such as closing the quantum metrology triangle.

Development of wideband impedance measurement services requires reference standards that can be characterized over the impedance and frequency ranges of interest. NIST has developed a system to characterize commercial four-terminal-pair capacitance standards from 1 pF to 1 nF over the frequency range from 1 kHz to 10 MHz. A bootstrapping technique using an LCR meter and an inductive voltage divider can extend the characterization to higher-valued capacitance standards up to 10 μF.

Major Accomplishments

- Developed a DSP-based signal generator that can be phase and frequency locked to a Josephson source, enabling the development of a quantum electrical power standard.
- Developed concept for new calculable capacitor based on laser frequency combs.
- Developed a programmable capacitance standard to provide capacitance values from 100 pF to 10 μF with a resolution of 1 pF.
- Orchestrated and led a capacitance key comparison for many countries in South, North, and Central America.

Selected Publications

- B. C. Waltrip, B. Gong, T. L. Nelson, C. J. Burroughs, A. Rüfenacht, S. P. Benz, P. D. Dresselhaus, Y. Wang, "Ac Power Standard Using a Programmable Josephson Voltage Standard," IEEE Transactions on Instrumentation and Measurement (2009, accepted)
- Y. Wang, R. D. Lee, L. Lu, J. Lawall, A. Chijioke, "Next-Generation Calculable Capacitor Using a Tunable-Laser Interferometer," Digest of Conference on Precision Electromagnetic Measurements (CPEM 2008), Broomfield, Colorado (2008)
- R. D. Lee, Y. Wang, G. J. FitzPatrick, "3-d Field Simulation to Design a Calculable Capacitor," Digest of Conference on Precision Electromagnetic Measurements (CPEM 2008), Broomfield, Colorado (2008)

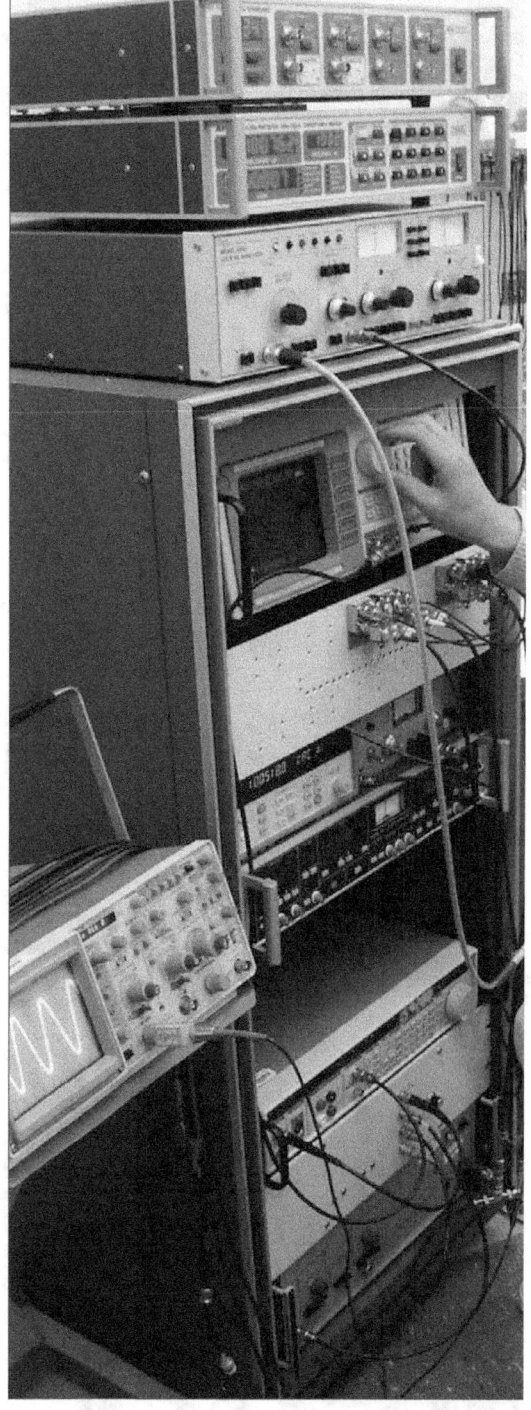

Figure 1. Setting up an automated system for determining the frequency dependence of fused-silica capacitors.

Figure 2. Performing a special test for a four-terminal-pair capacitance standard.

Contact

Yicheng Wang

(301) 975-4278

ywang@nist.gov

ELECTRONIC KILOGRAM

Summary

The unit of mass is still defined for the world by a 1 kg lump of metal kept in Paris, France. This artifact mass standard is suffering from 120 years of wear and contamination, so its value over time is becoming uncertain at several parts in 10 . While this is a very small amount of change, it has great implications for deterring the values of science's fundamental constants. As a potential replacement, the Electronic Kilogram Project compares the energy in power generated by mechanical and electrical means. Einstein's famous equation E=mc relates this energy measurement to mass. The electronic kilogram will define mass in terms of quantum mechanical systems similar to the second (atomic clocks) and the meter (laser wavelength), which are all unchanging in time.

Description

NIST has led the world since 1998 with three consistent results for the determination of Planck's constant (a fundamental constant related to mass). The most recent NIST value reported in 2005 has the lowest uncertainty so far, at 36 parts in 109. Two results from the National Physical Laboratory (NPL) in England and one from the Avogadro International Consortium have varied by 300 and 1000 parts in 10^9, respectively. This shows that significant progress has been made since the first NPL result in 1988, but also shows how difficult and complicated this experiment is.

Four international laboratories besides NIST are working with the same technique. In the experiment, a mass balance uses a precisely aligned induction coil in a high-stability magnetic field, where a current applied to the coil provides an electromagnetic force in opposition to the gravitational attraction on a mass standard. As a necessary and complementary measurement, the coil is moved to generate a voltage while recording the coil velocity. The reference quantities of mass, time, length, voltage, and resistance are based on in-lab peripheral systems: mass artifacts, GPS, laser interferometer, Josephson array volt system, and quantum Hall calibrated standard resistor.

Precise measurement, calibration, and other instrumentation issues must be well characterized, which is why this type of experiment is best and only performed at national standards laboratories. The International Committee for Weights and Measures (CIPM) has recommended a redefinition when the experiment proves its feasibility with several labs reproducing a consistent result within the present NIST uncertainty. With the next opportunity occurring in 2011, the race is on to improve the experiments and trigger a change in the International System of Units (SI) that will provide a quantum-based matrix of units for the foreseeable future, permanently stabilizing both scientific measurements and commercial standardization in production and trade of electrical, mass, and force measurement equipment.

Major Accomplishments

- Reported the lowest uncertainty in the world of 36 x 10^{-9} on a value of the Planck constant in 2005 that was consistent with original value reported in 1998.
- Publications of April 2005 Metrologia paper sparked CIPM decision to consider redefinition of kilogram.

Selected Publications

- R. Steiner, E. Williams, R. Liu, D. Newell, "Uncertainty Improvements of the NIST Electronic Kilogram," IEEE Trans. on Instrum. and Meas., vol. 56, no. 2, pp. 592-596 (2007)
- M. Mills, P. J. Mohr, T. J. Quinn, B. N. Taylor, E. R. Williams, "Redefinition of the Kilogram, Ampere, Kelvin and Mole: a Proposed Approach to Implementing CIPM Recommendation 1 (CI-2005)," Metrologia, vol. 43, no. 3, pp. 227–46 (2005)
- M. Mills, P. J. Mohr, T. J. Quinn, B. N. Taylor, E. R. Williams, "Redefinition of the Kilogram: a Decision Whose Time Has Come," Metrologia, vol. 42 no. 2, pp. 71-80 (2005)

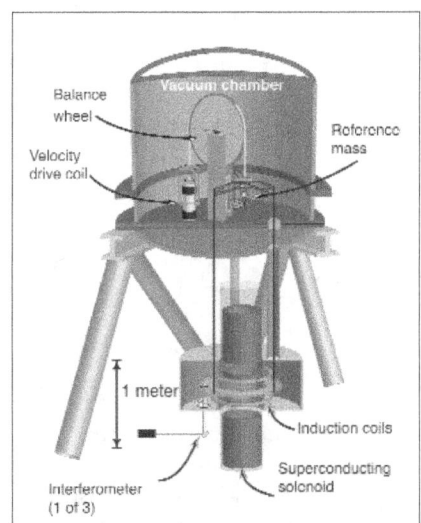

Figure 1.
Artifact International Prototype Kilogram (IPK).

Figure 2.
NIST Electronic Kilogram.

Figure 3.
Time comparison of scatter in the IPK copies versus the present scatter in NIST e-kilogram data.

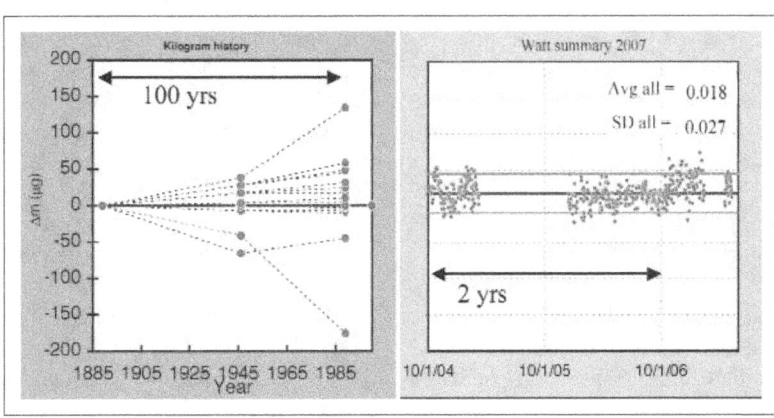

Contact

Richard Steiner

(301) 975-4226

richard.steiner@nist.gov

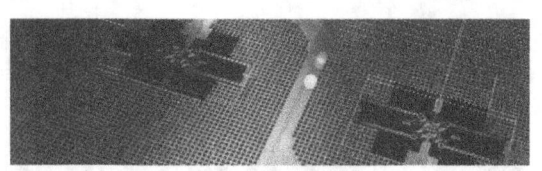

ELECTRIC POWER METROLOGY
AND THE SMART GRID

Summary

Our country's way of life depends on the electric power distribution system. Keeping the national electric grid in good working order – and ensuring power is measured accurately and billed fairly – requires a set of standards for electric power measurements. NIST is deeply involved in developing and maintaining these standards. Our efforts include devising metrology that allows new technologies to connect into existing power production and delivery systems, as well as standards that protect the infrastructure from potential dangers introduced by deregulation. This project's work also supports the realization of the Smart Grid, the future model of the U.S. electric power grid that incorporates cutting-edge technologies to achieve unprecedented efficiency, reliability, and safety.

Description

Power outages are at a minimum an inconvenience, but extended periods without power can be life-threatening; e.g., to patients in hospitals and during extreme weather. Deregulation of the U.S. electric power industry has complicated the task of ensuring the dependability of the nation's complex power infrastructure. NIST performs invaluable research that supports reliable power delivery, public safety, and accurate pricing of electric power. Ironically, modern technological advances are making this task even more difficult. For example, sensors and actuators used to control the operation of electric power systems are now widely connected via modems and the Web, but because they are designed for speed and other functional considerations rather than security, they may be vulnerable to attack. In conjunction with utilities and vendors, NIST researchers are identifying these weaknesses and reviewing the standards affected by them.

Deregulation has also opened the door to suppliers using non-traditional electricity generation technologies (such as wind and solar) that may introduce distortions into the flow of power delivered to customers. EEEL is developing systems to characterize the distortions and verify that meters can still operate accurately even when these distortions are present.

Modern society's embrace of more efficient electrical devices is also driving new standards research. To encourage reductions in electric power consumption, the U.S. Department of Energy (DOE) designates minimum efficiencies for electrical equipment, such as power transformers and electric motors. NIST advises DOE by developing technically sound sampling strategies and instrumentation for testing these devices.

To remain competitive in the global power market, U.S. industry needs standards that are internationally acceptable. International comparisons are essential for the validation of measurement techniques used at National Metrology Institutes across the globe and also for transnational sales of electric power.

Major Accomplishments

- Developed hardware and software to test more secure electric power control system communication techniques and to make sure that these techniques meet the relevant standards.
- Orchestrated, led, and analyzed a comparison of electric power measurements among countries that participate in the Interamerican Metrology System (SIM; North, South, and Central America).
- Performed essential electric power metrology for the Smart Grid, a model for the modernization of electric power production and distribution. The Smart Grid will be more reliable, efficient, and safer than today's grid.

Selected Publications

- B. C. Waltrip, B. Gong, T. L. Nelson, C. J. Burroughs, A. Rüfenacht, S. P. Benz, P. D. Dresselhaus, Y. Wang, "Ac power Standard Using a Programmable Josephson Voltage Standard," IEEE Transactions on Instrumentation and Measurement (2009, accepted)

Figure 1. Calibrating a Phasor Measurement Unit (PMU).

Contact

Thomas Nelson

(301) 975-2986

thomas.nelson@nist.gov

QUANTUM SENSORS

Summary

The ability to accurately measure the energy of photons from the infrared to gamma rays enables amazing scientific applications, from probing the origins of the universe to detecting terrorist activities. The Quantum Sensors Project develops sensors based on quantum phenomena for spectroscopy, imaging, and other precision measurements. EEEL integrates these sensors with custom superconducting and room-temperature electronics, cryogenic structures, and software to create complete measurement systems. Working with collaborators in industry, academia, and other government agencies, EEEL applies this measurement capability to applications including materials analysis, particle physics, nuclear nonproliferation and forensics, astronomy, cosmology, and homeland defense.

Description

The Quantum Sensors Project is a world leader in developing new detector systems. Project researchers have developed transition edge sensors (TES) for use in a variety of applications. These devices utilize a strip of superconducting material, biased in its transition from normal to superconducting states, as an extremely sensitive thermometer. This thermometer is attached to an absorber that is isolated from a cold (100 mK) heat sink by a micromachined structure. The heat deposited by incident photons is then measured to accurately determine their energy. These TES detectors and superconducting quantum interference device (SQUID) readout circuits are designed, fabricated, and implemented for use by a variety of different scientific and technical communities.

One example is the development of gamma-ray and alpha-particle detectors based on TES technology that have more than 10 times better energy resolution than conventional detectors. These detectors can resolve more lines in the complicated gamma-ray spectra of nuclear materials such as uranium and plutonium isotopic mixtures. The gamma-ray devices are being developed specifically to help in the verification of international nonproliferation treaties, by determining the plutonium content of spent nuclear fuel. The alpha-particle devices have similarly impressive performance and have demonstrated the ability to analyze mixed-actinide samples. These detectors are being developed for use in nuclear forensics. Prototypes of both systems have been delivered to our collaborators at Los Alamos National Laboratory. In the infrared regime, our TES bolometers have achieved world-record sensitivity. This impressive result confirms the utility of TES technology for this application as well. We are actively collaborating with many groups and are providing either detectors or superconducting readout and multiplexing circuits to many infrared and sub-millimeter instruments. Most recently, our detector efforts are focused on developing new polarization-sensitive bolometers for cosmic microwave background measurements.

Major Accomplishments

- Delivered gamma-ray and alpha-particle spectrometer systems to Los Alamos National Laboratory for development of nuclear forensic methods.
- Achieved world-record alpha-particle spectral resolution using TES detectors.
- Delivered detector and multiplexer components to several astronomical instruments including the Atacama Cosmological Telescope, SCUBA-2, SPIDER, and the South Pole Telescope.
- Designed, fabricated, and tested polarization-sensitive pixels suitable for cosmic microwave background measurements.
- Demonstrated (with Konrad Lehnert, Physics Laboratory) parametric amplifiers with sub-quantum noise-squeezed behavior.

Selected Publications

- R. D. Horansky, J. N. Ullom, J. A. Beall, G. C. Hilton, K. D. Irwin, D. E. Dry, E. P. Hastings, S. P. Lamont, C. R. Rudy, M. W. Rabin, "Superconducting Calorimetric Alpha Particle Sensors for Nuclear Nonproliferation Applications," Appl. Phys. Lett. 93, 123504, DOI:10.1063/1.2978204 (2008)
- J. A. B. Mates, G. C. Hilton, K. D. Irwin, L. R. Vale, K. W. Lehnert, "Demonstration of a Multiplexer of Dissipationless Superconducting Quantum Interference Devices," Appl. Phys. Lett. 92, 023514, DOI:10.1063/1.2803852 (2008)
- N. A. Miller, G. C. O'Neil, J. A. Beall, G. C. Hilton, K. D. Irwin, D. R. Schmidt, L. R. Vale, J. N. Ullom, "High resolution X-ray Transition-Edge Sensor Cooled By Tunnel Junction Refrigerators," Appl. Phys. Lett. 92, 163501, DOI:10.1063/1.2913160 (2008)

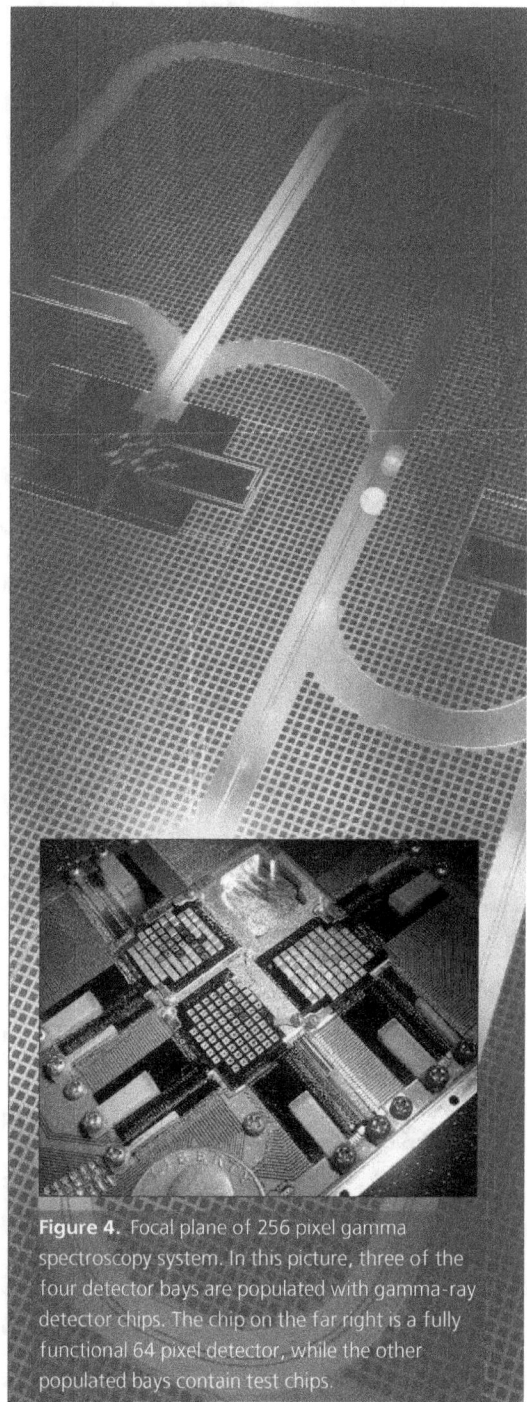

Figure 4. Focal plane of 256 pixel gamma spectroscopy system. In this picture, three of the four detector bays are populated with gamma-ray detector chips. The chip on the far right is a fully functional 64 pixel detector, while the other populated bays contain test chips.

Figure 1. SQUID-based multiplexer for SCUBA-2: This 1280 pixel (32 column x 40 row) multiplexer is used as the readout circuit for a submillimeter-wavelength astronomical camera for the SCUBA2 instrument currently operating on Mauna Kea in Hawaii.

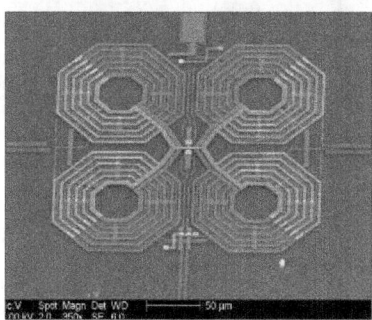

Figure 2. One pixel of a SQUID multiplexer readout circuit currently being used by a variety of astronomical instruments including the Atacama Cosmological Telescope in Chile.

Figure 3. Focal plane for BICEP-2, a 256-pixel polarimeter array being developed at JPL/Caltech with NIST SQUID multiplexers for deployment at the South Pole. Photos courtesy A. Turner (JPL) and J. Brevik (Caltech).

Contact

Kent Irwin

(303) 497-4991

kent.irwin@nist.gov

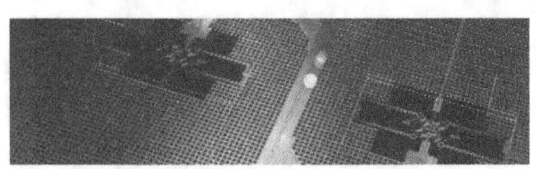

QUANTUM INFORMATION
AND MEASUREMENTS

Summary

America's future prosperity and security may rely in part on the exotic properties of quantum mechanics. Research on quantum information (QI) seeks to control and exploit these properties, and researchers are already generating "unbreakable" codes for ultra-secure encryption. They may someday build quantum computers that can solve problems in seconds that today's best supercomputers could not solve in years. This project applies the properties of a macroscopic quantum system, superconductivity, to the development of quantum bits (qubits), quantum circuits, and electrical measurement techniques that are limited only by the laws of quantum physics.

Description

NIST is home to a broad interdisciplinary program in quantum information science, which is exploring multiple implementations of qubits. The efforts include ion-trap quantum computing led by national Medal of Science Winner Dave Wineland, neutral atom quantum computing led by Nobel laureate Bill Philips, and quantum computing incorporating superconducting qubits led by Ray Simmonds of this project. Each of these approaches has associated advantages and challenges. Qubits made from ions and atoms are relatively easy to isolate from environmental influences and thus can maintain their coherence or stable quantum state for longer times. They are, however, more difficult to manipulate, and their properties are dictated by nature. Superconductivity can be used to create "artificial atoms" which are easy to connect to each other and manipulate but are more susceptible to decoherence by interaction with their environment. Work in this project falls into several areas: improving the performance of superconducting qubits by understanding the sources of decoherence and mitigating them, creating and demonstrating the elements of a quantum computer such as quantum memory and a quantum bus, investigating the interaction

("entanglement") of multiple quantum entities, probing at a fundamental level the limits which quantum phenomena place on electrical measurements, and creating instrumentation to approach these limits.

In concrete terms, this work includes theoretical investigations of interactions in qubits and single-charge devices as well as design, fabrication, and characterization of a wide variety of superconducting microdevices. In the qubit arena, we have significantly improved performance by modifying the device structure to reduce or remove dielectric materials (which contain naturally occurring or "rogue" qubits originating in atomic-level defects) from the circuits where possible and to substitute more defect-free materials where they cannot be removed. (Complementary work on quantum materials for qubits is being performed in the Quantum Magnetic Sensors and Materials Project.) In the instrumentation area, we have designed and demonstrated ultra-low-noise superconducting microwave amplifiers which have the promise to improve microwave measurements in a broad array of applications and potentially push these measurements to the quantum limit.

Major Accomplishments

- Demonstrated coherent quantum state storage and transfer between two phase qubits. Featured on the cover of *Nature*.
- Demonstrated DC SQUID microwave amplifier operating in the 7 GHz band with world record gain.
- Developed vacuum gap capacitors and crossovers and integrated them into superconducting qubits.
- Developed a resonator technique for evaluating qubit materials which allows rapid screen of candidate materials and fabrication methods.
- Performed seminal work on the role of quasiparticle poisoning in superconducting circuits which has had a major effect in redirection of qubit development.

Selected Publications

- M. A. Sillanpaa, J. I. Park, R. W. Simmonds, "Coherent Quantum State Storage and Transfer Between Two Phase Qubits Via a Resonant Cavity," Nature, Vol. 449, No. 7161, pp. 438-442 (2007)
- L. Spietz, K. Irwin, J. Aumentado, "Input Impedance and Gain of a Gigahertz Amplifier Using a DC Superconducting Quantum Interference Device in a Quarter Wave Resonator," Applied Physics Letters, Vol. 93, No. 8, pp. 082506-1-3 (2008)
- O. Naaman and J. Aumentado, "Poisson Transition Rates from Time-Domain Measurements with a Finite Bandwidth," J., Physical Review Letters, Vol. 96, No. 10, pp. 100201/1-4 (2006)

Figure 1. Depiction of a single microwave photon being transmitted between two superconducting qubit circuits, creating for the first time a "quantum electrical bus" between qubits that preserves and transfers the quantum state from one qubit to the other.

Figure 2. Micrograph of a superconducting qubit circuit that incorporates a unique vacuum gap capacitor to reduce dielectric decoherence in the circuit.

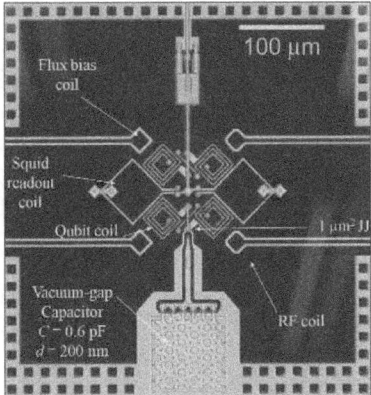

Contact

Bob Schwall

(303) 497-4732

robert.schwall@nist.gov

QUANTUM MAGNETIC
SENSORS AND MATERIALS

Summary

Ultra-sensitive magnetic sensors, quantum computers, and next-generation semiconductors all require the fabrication of extremely pure well-characterized materials. Quantum coherent materials show great promise for magnetic sensors as well as information processing technology. For magnetic sensors, spin-based transport in metals and across tunnel barriers is important because it increases the signal to noise and reduces the power. These devices have applications in a wide variety of fields, ranging from sensing to imaging. EEEL has developed large element arrays and systems to make forensic copies of magnetic tapes for data migration and authenticity analysis. In the area of quantum computing, EEEL is developing crystalline tunnel junctions that will improve quantum state visibility and measurements. EEEL is also working to improve the coherence of these devices by developing low-loss dielectrics.

Description

NIST is a world leader in the area of high-sensitivity magnetic field sensors. To achieve this, EEEL has explored spintronic devices, including anisotropic magneto-resistive (AMR) and tunneling magneto-resistive (TMR) devices. With the AMR devices, researchers developed tape read heads with many sensing elements. These devices are designed to operate at DC and are used to image magnetic tapes. A system was built for the FBI that is being validated for use on analog audio tape evidence. The TMR devices are targeted towards low-noise field sensors and are integrated with a flux concentrator. EEEL researchers have achieved noise levels better than one millionth of the Earth's magnetic field, with a sufficient dynamic range to run them in an unshielded environment. These devices are very low power and are targeted toward geological and exploratory work.

For quantum computing, EEEL is developing superconducting devices using a novel approach to making a tunnel barrier. Traditionally these tunnel junctions use convenient amorphous, thermal oxide barriers because the thickness is easily controllable, and they tend to be pin-hole free. However, it has been shown that these layers have energy-absorbing defects at random frequencies due to their amorphous nature. Therefore, EEEL developed a process to grow epitaxial tunnel junctions. This was challenging because the tunnel current depended exponentially on the barrier thickness, and epitaxial barriers require high temperatures to crystallize. Working around these issues using precision, ultra-high vacuum molecular beam epitaxy (MBE) growth, and lattice matched, superconducting rhenium films on sapphire substrates, EEEL is the first to be able to fabricate, characterize, and successfully integrate them into devices. In addition, the performance of the devices improved significantly, enabling us to use optical lithography rather than e-beam.

Major Accomplishments

- Developed low-noise magnetic field sensors applicable for geological applications.
- Developed magnetic imaging arrays and a system for conducting forensic analysis of magnetic tapes using this technology.
- Demonstrated the first implementation of epitaxial Josephson junction for quantum computing applications.
- Demonstrated that epitaxial Josephson junctions reduce the number of detrimental splittings in a solid state qubit.

Selected Publications

- F. C. S. da Silva, S. T. Halloran, A. B. Kos, D. P. Pappas, "256-Channel Magnetic Imaging System," Rev. Sci. Instrum. 79, 013709 (2008)
- S. Oh, K. Cicak, J. S. Kline, M. A. Sillanpää, K. D. Osborn, J. D. Whittaker, R. W. Simmonds, D. P. Pappas, "Elimination of Two Level Fluctuators in Superconducting Quantum Bits by an Epitaxial Tunnel Barrier," Phys Rev. B74 Rapid Communications, 100502® (2006)
- F. C. da Silva, S. T. Halloran, L. Yuan, D. P. Pappas, "A Z-Component Magnetoresistive Sensor," Applied Physics Letters 92, 142502 (2008)

Figure 1. One second of audio in a cassette tape imaged using the 256-sensor array showing: (I) regular audio signature, (II) erased region, and (III) erase head stop event. The white arrow between regions I and II indicates the erase mark starting point. The dotted rectangle highlights the erase stop event showed in detail in (b) and compared with the Bitter imaging technique (c). The black arrows indicate the recorder signature marks.

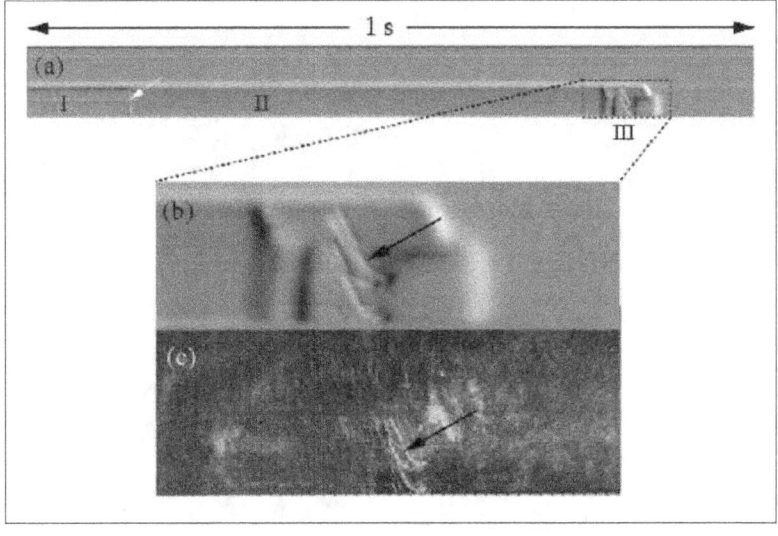

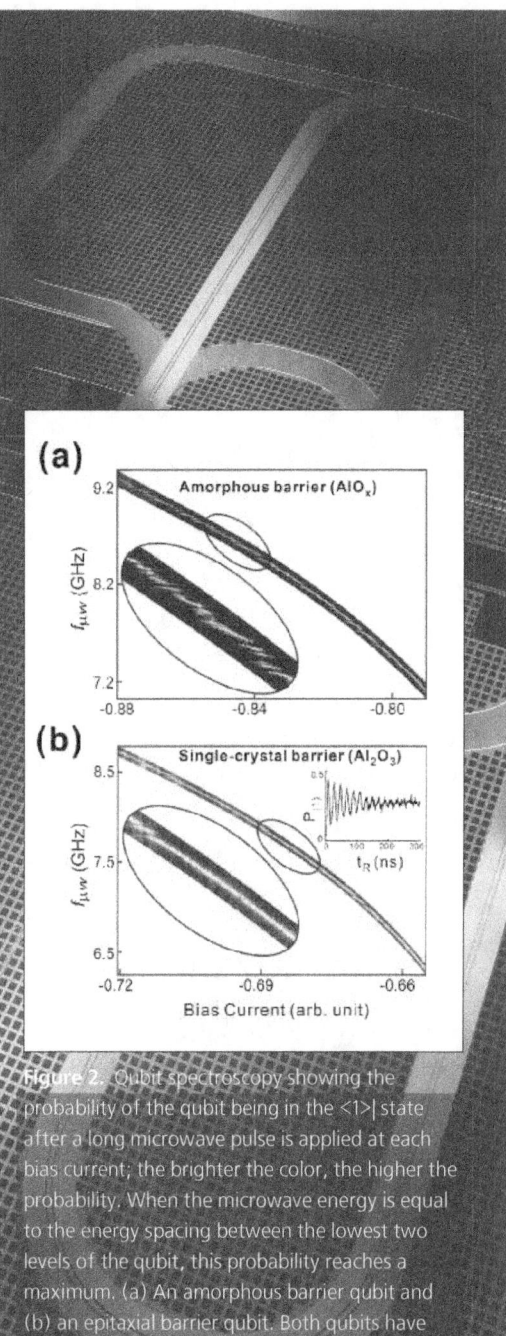

Figure 2. Qubit spectroscopy showing the probability of the qubit being in the $\langle 1|$ state after a long microwave pulse is applied at each bias current; the brighter the color, the higher the probability. When the microwave energy is equal to the energy spacing between the lowest two levels of the qubit, this probability reaches a maximum. (a) An amorphous barrier qubit and (b) an epitaxial barrier qubit. Both qubits have identical junction areas. The only difference is the trilayer structure.

Contact

David Pappas

(303) 497-3374

avid.pappas@nist.gov

ELECTROMAGNETICS
DIVISION

The Electromagnetics Division develops and promotes electromagnetic measurements, standards, and technology to support a broad range of technical needs. The Division's programs focus on accurate and reliable measurements throughout the radio spectrum. Key program directions include: (1) development of advanced measurement technologies required by both research-and-development and manufacturing communities; (2) the development and characterization of standard reference artifacts, measurement methods, and services that provide the basis for international recognition of measurements; and (3) the provision of expert technical support for national and international standards activities. Examples to indicate the breadth of areas influenced by our programs include high-speed microelectronics for computation and telecommunications, advanced antenna systems for applications in military radars and deep space communications, remote observation of the Earth's biosphere, acquisition and quantitative characterization of high-speed waveforms, medical diagnostic imaging, and reliable communications for our nation's emergency first-responders.

The Division's technical activities are organized into three research groups. The Radio-Frequency Electronics Group provides a broad range of state-of-the-art calibration services for fundamental radio-frequency and microwave quantities, which ensures that the U.S. scientific and industrial base has access to a measurement system that is reliable, accurate, and internationally accepted. In addition, this group extends new measurement tools and theories to higher operating frequencies, wider signal bandwidth, and smaller length scales. These are required for next-generation applications in microelectronics, high-speed communications, computing, and data storage. This group also develops new methods to measure the electromagnetic properties of materials and understand the interactions of electromagnetic waves with advanced materials.

The Radio-Frequency Fields Group develops theory and measurement techniques for the characterization of fundamental properties of advanced antenna systems and for the accurate measurement of electromagnetic fields. These capabilities are applied to the measurement of emissions and susceptibilities of electronic systems and devices. Of growing interest is the development of advanced measurement methods to characterize complex modulated telecommunication signals and to study the challenges faced by advanced communications when operated in complex real-world environments.

The Magnetics Group performs advanced research on fundamental aspects of magnetism and magnetodynamics, with particular focus on the behavior of nanoscale devices and systems for applications to magnetic sensors, magnetic information storage, and spintronics. This group also develops measurement technologies, methods and systems for quantitative biomagnetic imaging and "smart" magnetic contrast agents. In addition, this program maintains unique capabilities for the electromechanical characterization of superconductors, which enables large-scale applications of superconducting technologies.

ADVANCED HIGH-FREQUENCY
DEVICES

Summary

Ceaseless demand for increases in speed and integration of electronic devices drives a large segment of U.S. economic activity and impacts virtually every aspect of modern life, from improved medical diagnostics to faster computers to higher bandwidth communications. The operating frequencies of electronics are rapidly moving into the microwave frequency range and beyond, while integration requirements force device sizes down to the nanometer scale. This trend requires ever faster, more sensitive, and less invasive characterization techniques and creates entirely new measurement challenges related to strong interactions among devices and with the local environment. Further progress in the incorporation of novel nanotechnologies into electronics and communications applications is contingent on the development of high-frequency metrology at the nanoscale to define the relevant technical barriers and develop strategies to overcome them. The Advanced High-Frequency Devices Program develops measurement techniques and devices for characterizing nanoscale structures relevant for beyond CMOS electronics, high-frequency bioelectronic applications, and localized electromagnetic-field imaging.

Description

The primary goal of this program is metrology that enables advanced high-frequency device (electronics) development. Based on current trends in high-frequency electronics, the program is focused on metrology for two classes of devices: (1) high-frequency nanoscale devices (bringing high-frequency to the nanoscale) and (2) high-frequency devices based on novel materials (bringing high-frequency to new materials).

By learning how to fabricate and measure specific devices, this program develops metrology that is broadly applicable to whole classes of devices. The electronics research-and-development community of industry, government, and academia needs the metrological tools that are being developed to discern which high-frequency device paradigms they should pursue and which they should abandon. The impact of these developments on the electronics industry will be immense. Several industrial consortia have been created just to pursue research on advanced devices. On the one hand they recognize that quantitative measurement will make a major contribution to these efforts. On the other hand, these industrial entities are not able to clearly articulate their measurement needs. In addition to clarifying and providing the measurement methods, work in this field will enable new functionality that goes beyond conventional electronics. The initial investment in this area has yielded several specific achievements: broadband characterization of nanotubes, advances in near-field microwave microscopy, and superconducting microwave power limiters. External agencies, including the Defense Advanced Research Projects Agency (DARPA) and the Office of Naval Research (ONR), have recognized the value of this program and have invested accordingly. Over the course of the next 5 to 10 years, we will build on established measurement techniques to apply high frequency electromagnetic metrology to nanoscale devices for electronic and biological systems.

Major Accomplishments

- Designed, fabricated, measured, modeled, and performed error analysis for two-port, high-frequency, GaN nanowire devices.
- Developed a full model for characterization of nanoscale two-port devices. The model includes device characteristics as well as contact impedance.
- Performed broadband measurements of $SrTiO_3$ thin films at room temperature. These are the basis for a book chapter on challenges in thin-film measurements.
- Developed integrated microelectronic-microfluidics measurement structures for broadband electromagnetic characterization of picoliter fluid volumes.

Selected Publications

- T. Wallis, A. Imtiaz, H. Nembach, P. Rice, P. Kabos, "Metrology for High-Frequency Nanoelectronics," 2007 International Conference on Frontiers of Characterization and Metrology for Nanoelectronics (formerly, Characterization and Metrology for ULSI Technology), Gaithersburg, MD (2007)
- N. Orloff, J. Mateu, M. Murakami, I. Takeuchi, J. C. Booth, "Broadband Characterization of Multilayer Dielectric Thin-Films," 2007 IEEE MTT-S International Microwave Symposium, Honolulu, HI (2007)
- J. C. Booth, N. Orloff, J. Mateu, "Nonlinear Effects in Thin-Film Ferroelectric Transmission Lines at Microwave Frequencies," Proc. International Symposium on Applications of Ferroelectrics, Santa Fe, NM (2008)

Figure 1. On-wafer nonlinear characterizations.

Contacts

Jim Booth
Phone: (303) 497-7900
james.booth@nist.gov

Pavel Kabos,
Phone: (303) 497-3997
pavel.kabos@nist.gov

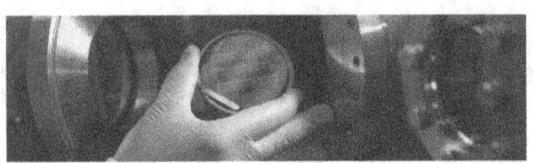

ADVANCED MATERIALS
METROLOGY

Summary

Everywhere around us are materials that are composed of tiny molecules and atoms that are influenced by invisible electromagnetic rays that travel as radio waves, microwaves, and sunlight. Just how these waves behave near and in materials has a strong influence on many areas of our life, from the TV we watch to devices in the doctor's office. Understanding and harnessing the interaction of microwaves with materials and the electrical properties of materials is very important to the development of new medical technologies and new electronics. The primary objectives of the Advanced Materials Metrology Program are to develop, improve, and analyze measurements of the electromagnetic properties of materials from the large–scale down to the nanoscale. The emphasis for the program is on measurement methods for substrates, thin films, liquids, biological materials, and artificial materials. Our program will advance the state of the art by introducing advanced concepts based on the underlying physics that govern the nature and properties of the materials.

Description

Over 100 years ago it dawned on scientists that a moving charge produced electromagnetic waves that traveled at the speed of light. Later it was found that these waves traveled as corpuscles called photons that interacted with materials. Electromagnetic devices cannot operate without the interaction of electromagnetic waves with materials, and the characterization of the interface between fields and materials will be a critical task for any device or metrology development from nanoscale to larger scales. EEEL areas of impact over the next 5 to 10 years will be developing measurements at frequencies approaching 1 terahertz, defining theoretical concepts, and developing the optimum measurement tools to extend electromagnetic metrology and reference materials to the nanoscale. We will develop quantitative electromagnetic measurements of thin-film electronic materials, liquids, biomaterials, and other advanced materials over a wide range of experimental conditions including frequency, temperature, and magnetic fields.

EEEL is performing state-of-the-art research that anticipates the measurement needs of industry years in advance in nondestructive substrate measurements, microfluidics, low- thin-film characterization, and near-field probing techniques. Industry, universities, other government laboratories, and standards committees have adopted many EEEL measurement methods. These include systems and test fixtures, best practices, and documentary standards. EEEL is expanding capabilities in advanced areas of near-field microwave microscopy, liquid characterization, and microfluidics.

The benefits of this work are many. Quantifying the interaction of electromagnetic fields with matter is a fundamental measurement challenge. This work directly benefits and leads basic research and development in microelectronics, biotechnology, and nanotechnology and influences a wide range of commercial, military, and homeland security applications.

Major Accomplishments

- Constructed and evaluated a liquid test fixture for the Transportation Security Administration (TSA).
- Completed a study of the interaction of radio-frequency to terahertz electromagnetic fields with material sizess from the macroscopic to nanoscale.
- Completed an electromagnetic analysis of near-field nanoscale probes.
- Completed an analysis of split-post and split-cylinder resonance techniques.
- Performed on-wafer metrology to study printed wiring board measurement problems.

Selected Publications

- J. Baker-Jarvis, M. D. Janezic, J. H. Lehman, "Dielectric-Resonator Method for Measuring the Electrical Conductivity of Carbon Nanotubes from Microwave to Millimeter Frequencies," Journal of Nanomaterials, vol. 2007, 12086 (2007)
- J. Baker-Jarvis, M. D. Janezic, D. Love, T. M. Wallis, C. L. Holloway, P. Kabos, "Phase Velocity in Resonant Structures," IEEE Transactions on Magnetics, vol. 42, pp. 3344-3346 (2006)
- M. Janezic, J. Jargon, J. R. Baker-Jarvis, "Relative Permittivity Measurements Using the Higher-Order Resonant Mode of a Near-Field Microwave Probe," International Union of Radio Science (URSI), Chicago, IL (2008)

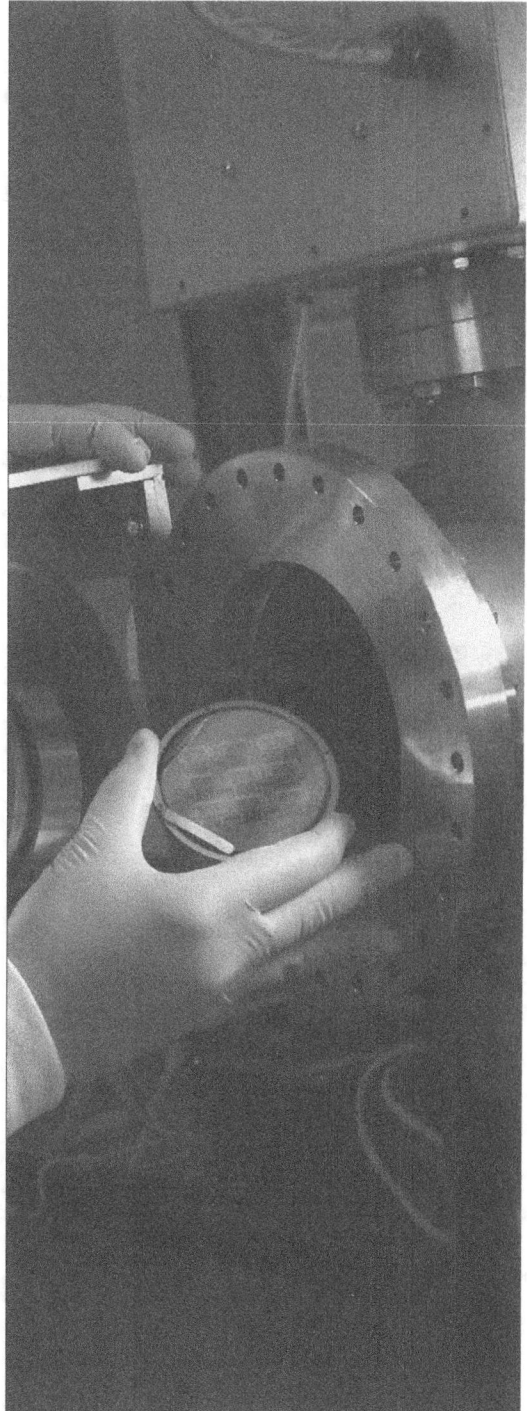

Figure 1. Dielectric measurement of liquids.

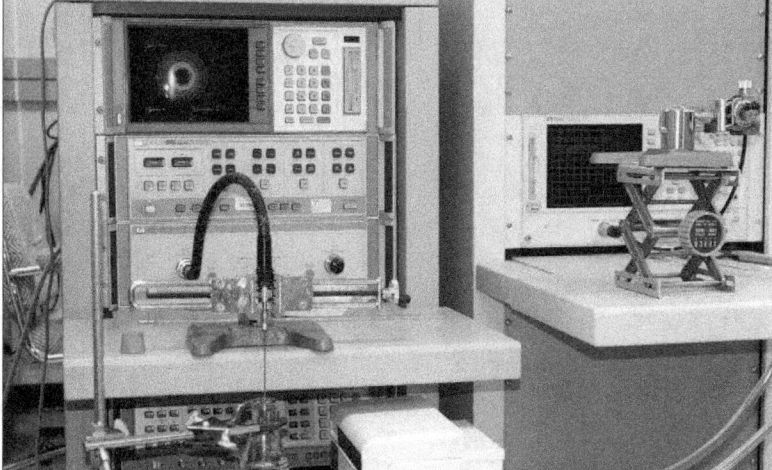

Contact

James Baker-Jarvis

(303) 497-5621

james.baker-jarvis@nist.gov

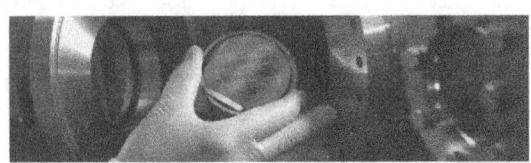

FUNDAMENTAL GUIDED-WAVE
METROLOGY

Summary

Information zips around inside modern personal computers at microwave frequencies. At these speeds, the information can interact with the materials of the computer chips and buses and possibly change in unexpected ways. These interactions must be measured and understood to keep computers functioning correctly, especially as they get smaller and faster. Helping computer chip manufacturers make these measurements is just one example of how the microwave standards and measuring techniques developed by the Fundamental Guided–Wave Metrology (FGWM) Program of EEEL supports industry. A common set of basic measurement capabilities and standards are necessary to support all these different users of RF and microwave devices. The FGWM Program develops and maintains the U.S. national standards for RF and microwave quantities, providing a wide range of state-of-the-art measurement capabilities and develops new measurement methods and systems. Everyday consumer devices (such as microwave ovens) as well as future advanced electronics systems are supported by the work of the FGWM Program.

Description

The number of devices that use microwaves is constantly growing. There is a constant push to use higher frequencies. Signals are becoming much more complex, including modulation effects, multiport/ differential signals, complex waveforms, and other unusual signal schemes. The capability to measure signals on integrated circuits is becoming critical for advanced devices. These new requirements are dictated by the needs of the telecommunication, computing, defense, and general electronics communities. EEEL's work looks at the fundamental measurement problems for microwave thermal noise, scattering-parameter, power, and waveform measurements. A large range of state-of-the-art microwave measurement capabilities, theoretical developments, techniques, and standards for customers are provided. The FGWM Program covers from 100 kilohertz to above 110 gigahertz.

The customers for the microwave measurement services come from a broad slice of the electronics industry. These customers generally use NIST measurements to support their internal calibration processes. This includes establishing their traceability, support for accreditation, calibration standards, and verification of their systems. The systems supported by these measurements may be anything from satellite systems to weapons or other military systems, computer chips, cell phones, or microwave ovens. One recent example is a calibration for the Food and Drug Administration (FDA) to support its microwave oven standards. The microwave measurement services are being transformed to better meet the needs of the program's customers. The FGWM Program is developing a strategy for moving the measurement services into the future and is developing improved methods for delivering the services. The main cornerstone of this approach is a strong research-and-development program in these areas. The measurement services are a natural outcome of the program's focus on the research of the fundamental metrology that underlies the measurement capabilities.

Electronics and Electrical Engineering Laboratory

Major Accomplishments

- Completed and evaluated a new WR-15 calorimeter for power measurements.
- Completed a 1.85 millimeter direct comparison power system and uncertainty analysis.
- Extended s-parameter capabilities to 1.85 millimeter connectors with uncertainty analysis.
- Constructed and tested a 400 gigahertz electro-optic sampling system.
- Terminated the classic artifact-based s-parameter measurement services. (These are being replaced with a measurement comparison approach.)

Selected Publications

- A. Lewandowski, D. Williams, "Characterization and Modeling of Random Vector Network Analyzer Measurement Errors," 17th International Conference on Microwaves, Radar and Wireless Communications (MIKON) (Warsaw, Poland), pp. 1-4 (2008)
- J. P. Randa, D. K. Walker, "On-Wafer Measurement of Transistor Noise Parameters at NIST," IEEE Transactions on Instrumentation and Measurement, vol. 56, pp. 551-554 (2007)
- D. Gu, D. Walker, J. P. Randa, "Noise-Parameter Measurement with Automated Variable Terminations," Conference on Precision Electromagnetic Measurements (CPEM), Broomfield, CO (2008)

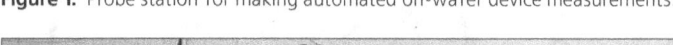

Figure 1. Probe station for making automated on-wafer device measurements.

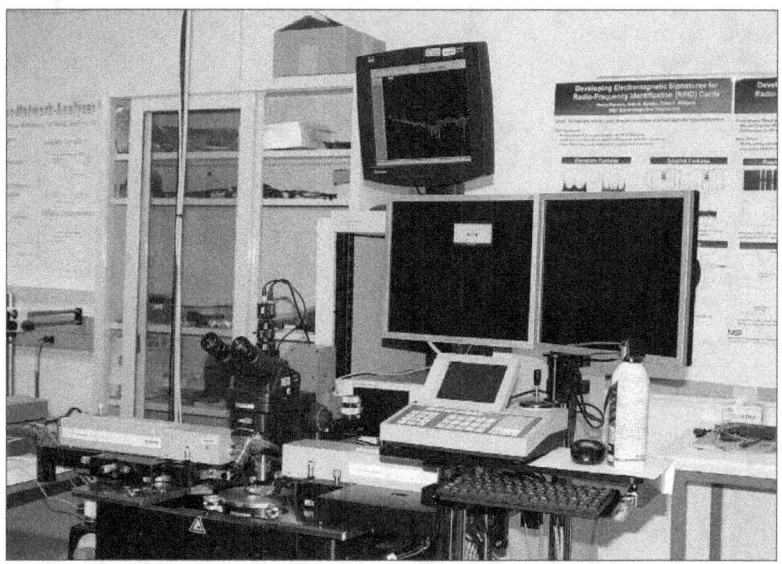

Contact

Ronald Ginley

(303) 497-5737

ronald.ginley@nist.gov

ANTENNA METROLOGY

Summary

Antennas are the eyes, ears, and voices of everything from cell phones to interplanetary spacecraft. The Antenna Metrology Program carries on EEEL's pioneering work on testing high-end antennas for critical hardware such as communications satellites, scientific spacecraft, radar, and aircraft. The program focuses on improving its near-field scanning method, which transforms measurements taken at centimeter distances into accurate predictions of an antenna's far-field, valid at distances of kilometers and beyond. Using mathematical tools developed at EEEL, the technique is used at hundreds of test ranges worldwide. Recent advances promise to extend the method's use.

Description

EEEL's Antenna Metrology Program has for three decades served companies and government agencies seeking to maximize the efficiency of communications, relying on the world's highest performance antennas. Program physicists and engineers are leaders in testing key antenna performance characteristics used in some of the world's most sensitive applications, such as those of radar and aircraft and of satellites and spacecraft vital for communications, weather prediction, and space science. Precise understanding of antenna performance enables designers of television satellites and spacecraft bound for other planets to avoid overbuilding antennas and related power sources, such as batteries and solar panels. They can thereby minimize spacecraft weight — and costs — where an incremental pound can cost $10,000 to launch. Equally important, proper testing of antennas on scientific spacecraft costing hundreds of millions of dollars provides assurance that precious data will make it back to Earth. EEEL scientists pioneered the near-field scanning technique — now the standard method for testing high-performance antennas designed to communicate across tens, thousands, or even millions of kilometers — and continue to advance it both theoretically and experimentally. The private sector and other government agencies provide most testing services based on EEEL's ground-breaking work. In hundreds of test ranges worldwide, engineers test antennas using probes designed to capture an antenna's output. In the U.S., each antenna probe is NIST-traceable, or NIST-calibrated. Such testing measures an antenna's near-field at close distances (a few centimeters), then uses mathematical algorithms developed at NIST to determine the far-field. Near-field scanning allows for accurate assessment of the gain (the amount of power transmitted or received in the antenna's primary direction), polarization (the orientation of the electromagnetic field), and pattern (the angular distribution of transmitted or received energy) of antennas operating at frequencies from 1.5 gigahertz to 110 gigahertz.

Project scientists recently scored a major success in the race to stay ahead of increasing antenna frequencies with their development of a dynamic laser-based antenna-probe tracking system with probe-position correction algorithms, which enable the use of existing near-field scanning ranges at much higher frequencies than previously attainable — thereby extending the life of some of the nation's key antenna-testing infrastructure. Such higher frequencies hold significant promise in the areas of medical and security imaging and radiometer systems for improved weather and climate prediction. Project scientists are also working on imaging applications that could one day pinpoint undesired electromagnetic reflections in test chambers, enabling even more accurate antenna calibration.

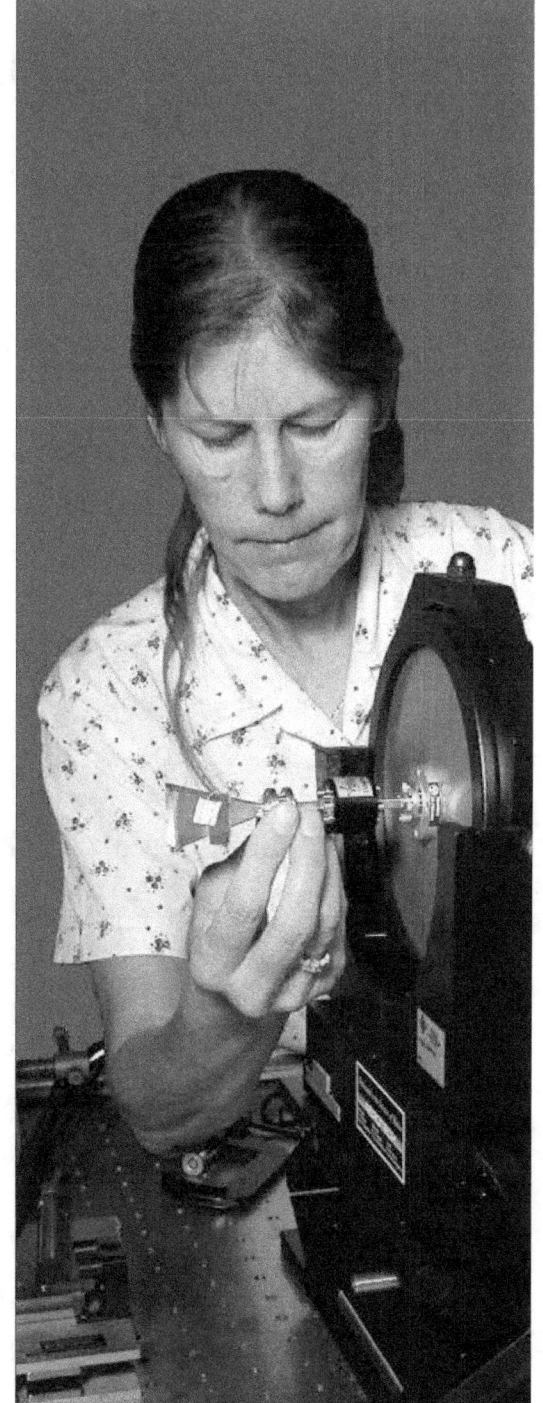

Major Accomplishments

- Completed and documented a method for estimating uncertainty due to the source of known brightness temperature being in the near-field of the radiometer.
- Determined gains and compared results of three antennas (one dual-port probe) using both the extrapolation and pattern integration methods.
- Established a test bed at 13.56 megahertz for testing radio-frequency identification (RFID) cards for load modulation (return signal strength) and durability when cards are exposed to electrostatic discharge or to high strength alternating electric and magnetic fields.

Selected Publications

- M. Francis, R. Wittmann, "Near-Field Scanning Measurements: Theory and Practice," in Modern Antenna Handbook, John Wiley, Ch. 19, pp. 929-976 (2008)
- R. Wittmann, M. Francis, R. Direen, "Chamber Imaging Using Near-Field Scanning," in Proc. 2008 IEEE Antennas and Propagation Symposium (San Diego, CA), ID 10.1109/APS.2008.4619141 (2008)
- J. Guerrieri, K. MacReynolds, M. Francis, R. Wittmann, D. Tamura, "Planar Near-Field Measurement Results Up To 94 GHz Using Probe Position Correction," in Proc. 27th AMTA Symposium (Newport, RI), pp. 110-116 (2005)

Figure 1.
The EEEL millimeter-wave extrapolation range being prepared for antenna measurements.

Contact

Michael Francis

(303) 497-5873

michael.francis@nist.gov

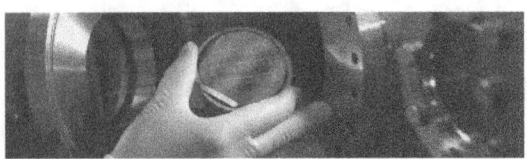

FIELD PARAMETER
METROLOGY

Summary

Consider the consequences if nearby electronics could interfere with a jet's instruments or cause an automobile to stall. The Electromagnetic Field Parameter Program develops ways of measuring electromagnetic (EM) emissions and susceptibilities to electronic interference of electronic devices and systems. The program maintains the capability to provide EM field measurements. Applications include the communications needs of first-responders to emergencies, measurements of the shielding effectiveness of advanced materials, effects from and on other electronic components, the statistics of electromagnetic fields in rooms and buildings, and the effects on biological subjects.

Description

This program generates reference EM fields and calibrates EM probes required for their accurate measurement. Accurate EM field measurements are needed to characterize our wireless world and ensure that the valuable electromagnetic spectrum is optimally used, that electronic systems are compatible and neither sources nor victims of EM interference, and that people are not exposed to hazardous fields. As instrumentation and electronics achieve higher clock rates, EM field parameter metrology is needed at ever higher frequencies. The program is working to extend current methods and facilities to higher frequencies and develop new test methods to increase accuracy and reduce measurement costs.

The program is working on extending open area test site test methods to frequencies above the 1 gigahertz specified by most international electromagnetic compatibility (EMC) standards. Fully anechoic chambers are accepted as standard sites for approximate free-space measurements. Time domain methods are being studied as a way to measure the characteristics of these rooms and to improve the results obtained therein. This type of chamber is also being

evaluated for EMC product testing up to 40 gigahertz. Closed test systems such as transverse EM cells have been widely adopted for testing small antennas, sensors, and probes, but are normally limited by geometrical constraints to below 1 gigahertz. EEEL recently finished construction and testing of a new closed-cell co-conical geometry system that can be used to test such devices up to 45 gigahertz. This new test fixture reduces test times from weeks to hours.

The program provides information to standards organizations to help correlate measurements between various EMC test facilities. The program also cooperates with the national test laboratories of our international partners to perform round-robin testing and comparison of standard antennas and probes. This assures international agreement in their performance and reduces the uncertainties in the areas of metrology that affect international trade. The program's goal is to develop and evaluate reliable and cost-effective standards, test methods, and measurement services related to complex EM fields for EMC of electronic devices and other applications in health, defense, and homeland security.

Major Accomplishments

• Completed a co-conical field generation system (CFGS) for the Air Force. The CFGS will reduce hazard probe calibration times from weeks to hours.

• Completed and documented high-intensity radiated field (HIRF) shielding effectiveness tests on representative commercial aircraft (Boeing 737-200, Boeing 767-400ER, Bombardier Global 5000, Beechcraft Premier 1A Composite Business Jet); the results were delivered to the FAA.

• Described analytically and verified experimentally a new method to quantify the shielding effectiveness of physically small but electrically large enclosures (e.g., instrument and computer housings) in reverberation chambers; introduced the method into the applicable IEEE standard.

Selected Publications

• K. Remley, G. Koepke, C. Holloway, C. Grosvenor, D. Camell, J. Ladbury, D. Novotny, W. Young, G. Hough, M. McKinley, Y. Becquet, J. Korsnes, "Measurements to Support Broadband Modulated-Signal Radio Transmissions for the Public-Safety Sector," NIST Technical Note 1546 (2008)

• C. Grosvenor, D. Camell, G. Koepke, D. Novotny, R. Johnk, "Electromagnetic Airframe Penetration Measurements of a Beechcraft Premier 1A," NIST Technical Note 1548 (2008)

• D. Camell, R. Johnk, D. Novotny, C. Grosvenor, "Free-Space Antenna Factors Through the Use of Time-Domain Signal Processing," in Proc. 2007 IEEE International Symposium on Electromagnetic Compatibility (Honolulu, HI), pp. 1-5 (2007)

Figure 1. The co-conical field generation system developed by EEEL in preparation for testing.

Contact

Galen Koepke

(303) 497-5766

galen.koepke@nist.gov

WIRELESS SYSTEMS
METROLOGY

Summary

Imagine how much safer a fire fighter's job would be if it were possible for a robot to navigate in a burning building and locate those in need of assistance.
The Wireless Systems Metrology Program develops ways to measure complex telecommunication signals used by industry, public safety (rescue workers), and government.
The program develops methods to measure communication and data signals and to imitate complex environments where reliable reception may be a problem.
Applications include developing tests to evaluate the effects of interference on wireless communications used in factories for the control of robots, methods to measure cellular telephone fields, test facilities for evaluating search and rescue communications, and robot communications.

Description

The Wireless Systems Metrology Program supports the growing wireless industry by developing methods to test the operation and functionality of wireless devices in the presence of various types of distortion. This includes multipath distortion, ranging from a line-of-sight environment (low-multipath) to a pure Rayleigh environment (high-multipath).

The Wireless Systems Metrology Program is also concerned with the impact of nonlinear distortion on the transmission of wireless signals, which can be especially severe for new wideband modulated signal transmissions. Accurately measuring distortion behavior of nonlinear radio-frequency devices is a key element in understanding how the device will perform once it is incorporated into a system. Even under weakly nonlinear conditions, low-noise devices such as those used in receiver front ends will exhibit nonlinear behavior that includes harmonic generation and intermodulation distortion. The program has studied problems that commonly arise in performing and interpreting nonlinear measurements, such as power- and wave-based representations and the effects of terminating impedance on intermodulation distortion. Researchers are also working to develop traceability to fundamental parameters such as power and electric field.

Major Accomplishments

- Demonstrated that a reverberation chamber can be used to generate a variable multipath environment, which allows wireless devices to be tested in the laboratory rather than in field tests.
- Developed standards to ensure reliable wireless communications for emergency responders in difficult radio environments.
- Assisted the National Institute of Environmental Health Sciences, which is conducting a long-term animal study to evaluate health risks associated with cellular telephone fields, by testing the performance of 21 reverberation chambers that will be utilized in the study.

Selected Publications

- E. Genender, C. Holloway, K. Remley, J. Ladbury, G. Koepke, H. Garbe, "Using a Reverberation Chamber to Simulate the Power Delay Profile of a Wireless Environment," in Proc. 2008 EMC Europe Symposium (Hamburg, Germany), pp. 219-224 (2008)
- K. Remley, G. Koepke, C. Grosvenor, R. Johnk, J. Ladbury, D. Camell, J. Coder, "NIST Tests of the Wireless Environment in Automobile Manufacturing Facilities," NIST Technical Note 1550 (2008)
- K. Remley, G. Hough, G. Koepke, R. Johnk, D. Camell, C. Grosvenor, "Wireless Communications in Tunnels for Urban Search and Rescue Robots," in Proc. 2008 Performance Metrics for Intelligent Systems, Gaithersburg, MD (2008)

Figure 1. EEEL staff measure the wireless communication link environment in an automotive factory.

Contact

Catherine Remley

(303) 497-3652

catherine.remley@nist.gov

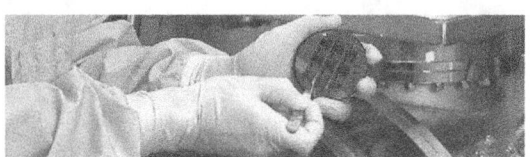

NANOMAGNETICS

Summary

Hard-disk drives in personal computers continue to become smaller, faster, and cheaper. These magnetic devices push the limits of technology, with current data bit densities of 50 billion per square centimeter.
The magnetic orientation of thin films in write heads, read heads, and recording media all switch extremely quickly. The Nanomagnetics Program investigates the high-frequency behavior of nanoscale magnetic materials and devices. The switching of magnetization at frequencies in the hundreds of megahertz to hundreds of gigahertz will be the foundation for future magnetic data storage systems and microwave integrated circuits. These technologies will depend on newly discovered properties and limitations of magnetic materials and devices that appear only at the nanoscale.

Description

Future computer hard disk drives are likely to require patterned media composed of uniform, perpendicularly magnetized nanodots instead of present-day continuous magnetic films. EEEL has demonstrated that the magnetic fields required to switch the magnetization of nanodots is critically dependent on the quality of their edges. EEEL is developing new, highly sensitive, magneto-optic instruments to measure the dynamics of magnetic nanodots as a function of frequency, with the goal of evaluating nanodot quality and homogeneity via a rapid spectroscopic analysis of individual nanodots.

Spintronics exploits the interaction between electrons' spin angular momentum and the magnetization of a film. EEEL developed the first microwave spin-transfer nano-oscillators based on point current contacts to planar films. These oscillators have very sharp resonant frequencies. EEEL showed how signals emitted by multiple nano-oscillators will naturally synchronize, coherently combining their outputs and stabilizing their oscillation frequency. EEEL explained the mechanism responsible for nano-oscillator coupling and solved a potential barrier to widespread application by demonstrating how oscillations can be made to occur in a zero applied magnetic field.

In addition to oscillators, electron spin torque may be used to switch future nonvolatile magnetic random-access memory (MRAM) elements. Compared to switching memory bits with magnetic fields, this method would offer higher speed, greater reliability, and lower power, and it is scalable to smaller device dimensions. EEEL is developing methods to measure the switching behavior of prototype spin-MRAM.

Imperfections in magnetoresistive sensors give rise to random magnetic fluctuations, which limit their sensitivity. EEEL has obtained evidence of these stochastic processes in the form of electron microscope images of magnetic domain fluctuations in active devices. EEEL has fabricated improved magnetic tunnel-junction sensors by annealing them in high fields in a reducing environment and by using magnetic flux concentrators.

Major Accomplishments

- Determined that magnetic reversal in perpendicularly magnetized nanostructures is highly dependent on the nature and condition of the edges.
- Determined that spin-transfer-driven oscillations in nanocontacts made to spin-valve structures can occur in zero field, which will enable applications such as on-chip timing and signal processing.
- Demonstrated mutual phase-locking of microwave spin-torque nano-oscillators. Spin waves, rather than magnetic fields, are the primary interaction mechanism.
- Identified sources of 1/f noise and time-dependent nanoscale fluctuations in magnetic films. Imaged magnetic fluctuations in active magnetic sensors.

Selected Publications

- T. J. Silva and W. H. Rippard, "Developments in Nano-Oscillators Based Upon Spin-Transfer Point-Contact Devices," Journal of Magnetism and Magnetic Materials, vol. 320, pp. 1260-1271 (2008)
- W. H. Rippard and M. R. Pufall, "Microwave Generation in Magnetic Multilayers and Nanostructures," in Handbook of Magnetism and Advanced Magnetic Materials, John Wiley, Sussex, U.K. (2007)
- R. Heindl, S. E. Russek, T. J. Silva, W. H. Rippard, J. A. Katine, and M. J. Carey, "Size Dependence of Intrinsic Spin Transfer Switching Current Density in Elliptical Spin Valves," Applied Physics Letters, vol. 92, 262504 (2008)

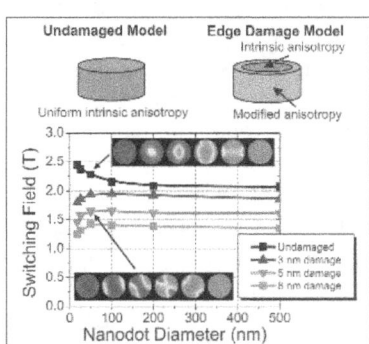

Figure 1. Top drawing: Schematic of a model used to include nanodot edge damage in micromagnetic simulations. Bottom graph: Diameter dependence of the switching field from simulations for various values of edge damage. The insets show the time evolution in a 50 nanometer nanodot as it undergoes reversal in the undamaged and edge-damaged cases over a time of approximately 1 nanosecond. The color scale represents the z-component of the magnetization.

Figure 2. Simulation showing spin-wave interaction between two spin-transfer oscillators. Focused ion beam cut breaks coupling. Oscillators phase-lock without the cut. The scanning electron micrograph shows actual device.

Figure 3. Simulation of magnetization for a 176 nanometer by 60 nanometer device. Colors represent the average x-axis magnetization (red positive, blue negative). Magnetic oscillations grow until device switches.

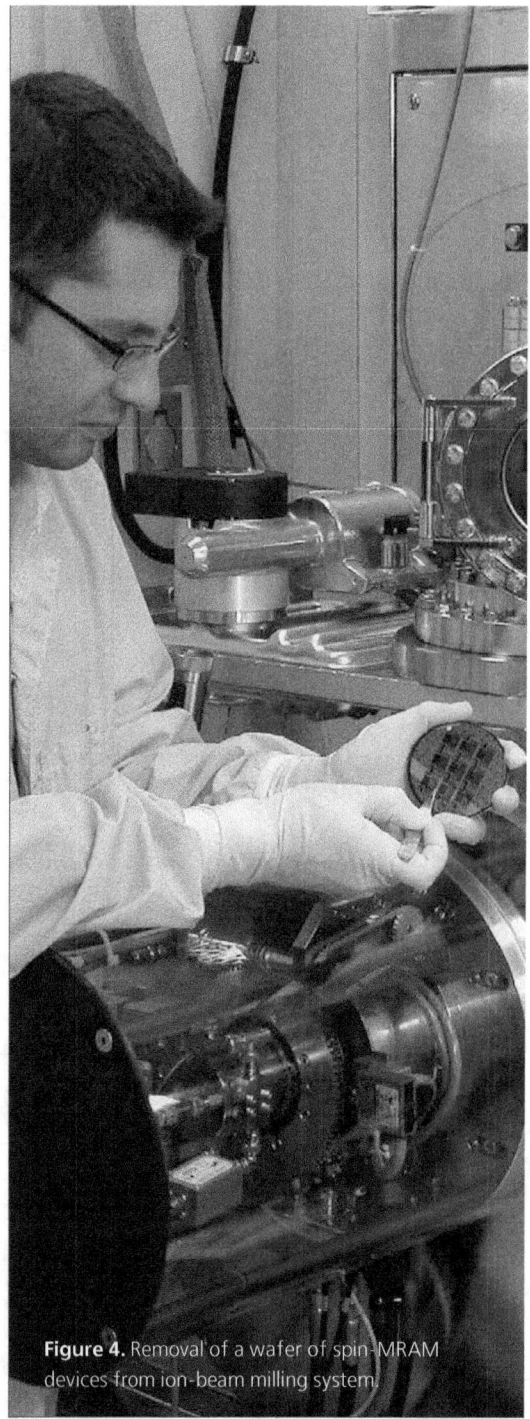

Figure 4. Removal of a wafer of spin-MRAM devices from ion-beam milling system.

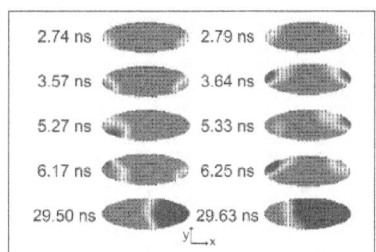

Contacts

Tom Silva
(303) 497-7826, thomas.silva@nist.gov

Bill Rippard
(303) 497-3882, william.rippard@nist.gov

Stephen Russek
(303) 497-5097, stephen.russek@nist.gov

BIOMAGNETICS

Summary

Magnetic resonance imaging (MRI) gives detailed medical images of the body's internal tissues and organs without the use of harmful radiation. MRI is based on magnetic vibrations of the protons in water. The Biomagnetics Program seeks to improve MRI through the invention of multifunctional magnetic contrast agents and the development of measurements and standards to make MRI quantitative and traceable, instead of qualitative and instrument dependent.

The Biomagnetics Program also develops terahertz detectors with unprecedented sensitivity and resolution for bio-imaging, identification of trace chemical molecules, and remote atmospheric sensing to monitor climate change. The imaging of malignant skin tumors by the passive detection of terahertz radiation is safe and painless.

Description

Customized microscopic magnets could add color and sensitivity to MRI. In collaboration with the National Institutes of Health (NIH), EEEL has shown how such micromagnets could act as "smart tags" to identify particular cells, tissues, or physiological conditions. Each micromagnet consists of two round, vertically stacked magnetic disks, a few micrometers in diameter, separated by a gap. Customized magnetic fields can be created by adjusting materials, gap, or disk thickness or diameter. The open design allows the diffusion of water through the micromagnet, producing a signal that may be thousands of times stronger than that produced by a similarly sized, but stationary, volume of water. The diffusion effectively increases local MRI sensitivity, which could lead to faster imaging, images that are richer in information, or reduced dose requirements for contrast agents. The micromagnets can be made using conventional microfabrication techniques and are compatible with standard MRI hardware.

In collaboration with a committee of the International Society for Magnetic Resonance in Medicine (ISMRM), EEEL is developing a standard "phantom" for the calibration of MRI machines.

Currently, MRI scanners drift over time, and different machines give different images. Quantitative, traceable MRI will provide accurate and consistent images, validate disease mechanisms and therapeutic outcomes, and facilitate the transition to computer-aided diagnostics. The pharmaceutical industry will use quantitative MRI to objectively test the efficacy of new drugs.

Biological and chemical samples naturally emit characteristic signatures of terahertz radiation, but detecting and measuring them is a challenge because the signals are weak and absorbed rapidly by the atmosphere. A prototype imager developed by EEEL uses a sensitive superconducting detector, microelectronics, and optics to operate in the terahertz range. The system can detect temperature differences smaller than 0.5 °C, which could differentiate between, for example, tumors and healthy tissue. The technique is sensitive enough to detect the weak terahertz signals naturally emitted by samples, eliminating the need to actively illuminate them. The technology may become a new tool for early tumor detection and rapid and precise identification of chemical hazards for homeland security.

Major Accomplishments

- Invented MRI contrast agents with spectral signatures based on the geometry of the magnetic microstructures.
- Developed and characterized a passive heterodyne hot electron bolometer imager operating at 850 gigahertz with spatial resolution of 4 millimeters.
- Showed that the efficiency of solutions of the single-molecule Fe-8 nanomagnet as an MRI contrast agent compared to that of a gadolinium chelate depends on concentration.
- Developed a novel platform for microfluidic manipulation of magnetic particles based on an array of magnetic spin valves with bistable ferromagnetic "on" and antiferromagnetic "off" states.

Selected Publications

- G. Zabow, S. Dodd, J. Moreland, A. Koretsky, "Micro-Engineered Local Field Control for High-Sensitivity Multispectral MRI," Nature, vol. 453, pp. 1058-1063 (2008)
- E. Gerecht, D. Z. Gu, L. X. You, K. S. Yngvesson, "A Passive Heterodyne, Hot Electron Bolometer Imager Operating at 850 GHz," IEEE Transactions on Microwave Theory and Techniques, vol. 56, pp. 1083-1091 (2008)
- B. Cage, S. E. Russek, R. Shoemaker, A. J. Barker, C. Stoldt, V. Ramachandaran, N. S. Dalal, "The Utility of the Single-Molecule Magnet Fe-8 as a Magnetic Resonance Imaging Contrast Agent Over a Broad Range of Concentration," Polyhedron, vol. 26, pp. 2413-2419 (2007)

Figure 3.
Heterodyne terahertz imaging and spectroscopy system
Image Copyright Geoffrey Wheeler, 2007

Figure 1. Scanning electron micrograph of engineered magnets, 3 micrometers in diameter, for enhanced MRI contrast.

Figure 2. Model of phantom under development by EEEL and the ISMRM Committee on Standards for Quantitative MRI. It will include traceable dimensions and magnetic contrast agents.

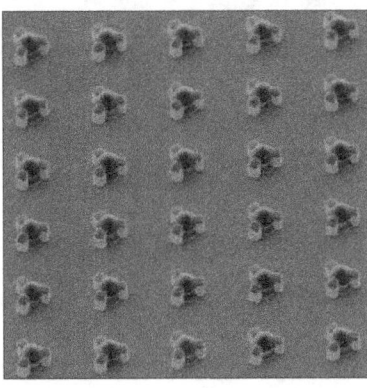

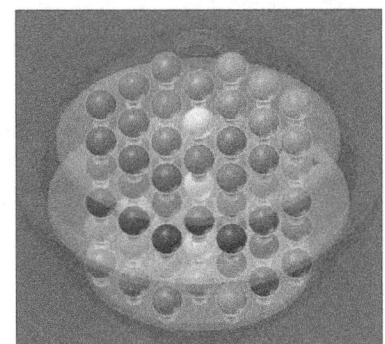

Contacts

John Moreland
(303) 497-3641
john.moreland@nist.gov

Stephen Russek
(303) 497-5097
stephen.russek@nist.gov

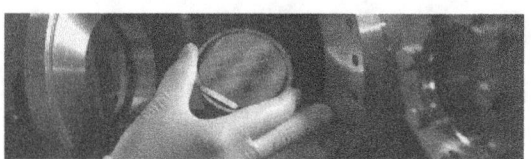

SUPERCONDUCTIVITY

Summary

Energy losses in the transmission of electricity from generation plants to cities amount to over five percent. Underground electrical distribution lines in cities are at the limits of their current-carrying capacities. These are examples of problems that could be mitigated with superconductors. The Superconductivity Program conducts enabling research in superconductivity for energy, power grid reliability, medical instruments, and fundamental physics. The program has a worldwide reputation for its measurements of the effects of mechanical strain and temperature on the ability of superconductor wires to carry extremely high current. Additionally, the program develops standard measurement techniques and international documentary standards for measurements to characterize superconductors. It provides quality assurance and reference data for commercial and prototype high-temperature and low-temperature superconductors.

Description

The global market for superconductors is about $5 billion, largely dominated by superconducting magnets for magnetic resonance imaging (MRI) machines. However, recent successful demonstration projects point to increasing applications in power transmission lines, fault current limiters, transformers, synchronous condensers, magnetic energy storage devices, and other components for the electrical power grid. Applications in proton radiation cancer treatments are also emerging. Measurements to characterize superconductors require specialized expertise, and the measurements must be reliable in order to solve engineering problems that prevent wider use of both conventional and high-temperature superconductors.

To further its unique role as the de facto reference laboratory for superconductor critical current measurements, the program recently developed the world's first high-current unified apparatus to measure critical current as a function of strain, temperature, and magnetic field. It is being used for fundamental research at NIST, the U.S. contribution to the International Thermonuclear Experimental Reactor (ITER), and in support of the Department of Energy's High-Energy Physics particle accelerator program. NIST's data on the irreversible strain limit and alternating-field losses of Nb_3Sn superconductor wires have already impelled ITER to change its wire specifications and heat-treatment schedule. The reason strain is such an important parameter is that, in most applications, superconductors are subject to powerful Lorentz forces due to the current they carry in the magnetic field of neighboring wires. These forces strain the wires, usually to their detriment.

Recent research in this program has shown that the reduction of critical current with compressive strain in the high-temperature Y-Ba-Cu-O superconductor, which is being developed for electric transmission lines, is intrinsic to the superconductor grains. In fact, the reversible strain effect in single-crystal thin films is comparable to that of multi-granular Y-Ba-Cu-O coated conductors. This could have profound implications for the development of practical high-temperature superconductors. The Superconductivity Program has developed an apparatus to measure the critical current of Y-Ba-Cu-O coated conductors as a function of strain, temperature, magnetic field, and magnetic field angle. Other research in support of the commercial development of high-temperature superconductors has shown how to prevent Y-Ba-Cu-O from delaminating from their metal substrates when under strain.

Major Accomplishments

- Designed and constructed a unified temperature-strain apparatus.
- Demonstrated that the reversible strain effect in Y-Ba-Cu-O is intragranular in origin.
- Developed a model to describe the reversible strain effect in Y-Ba-Cu-O grain boundaries.
- Constructed new electromechanical test structures for second-generation, high-temperature superconductors, including a new apparatus to measure the strain effect in variable magnetic-field angles.
- Showed how low irreversible strain limits could explain serious damage in ITER prototype magnets.
- Formulated a scaling law for the flux pinning force in MgB_2 superconductors.
- Updated 12 International Electrotechnical Commission (IEC) standards, including measures of uncertainty.

Selected Publications

- D. C. van der Laan, J. W. Ekin, "Large Intrinsic Effect of Axial Strain on the Critical Current of High-Temperature Superconductors for Electric Power Applications," Applied Physics Letters, vol. 90, 052506 (2007)
- N. Cheggour, J. W. Ekin, L. F. Goodrich, "Critical-Current Measurements on an ITER Nb_3Sn Strand: Effect of Axial Tensile Strain," IEEE Transactions on Applied Superconductivity, vol. 17, pp. 1366-1369 (2007)
- L. F. Goodrich, N. Cheggour, J. W. Ekin, T. C. Stauffer, "Critical-Current Measurements on ITER Nb_3Sn Strands: Effect of Temperature," IEEE Transactions on Applied Superconductivity, vol. 17, pp. 1398-1401 (2007)

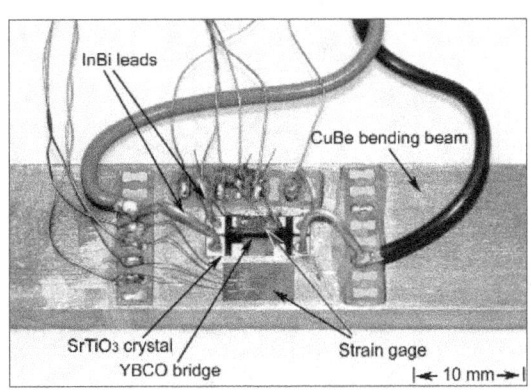

Figure 4. Critical-current measurement of a single-crystal thin film of Y-Ba-Cu-O deposited on a $SrTiO_3$ crystal. Axial compressive strain is applied by bending the beam.

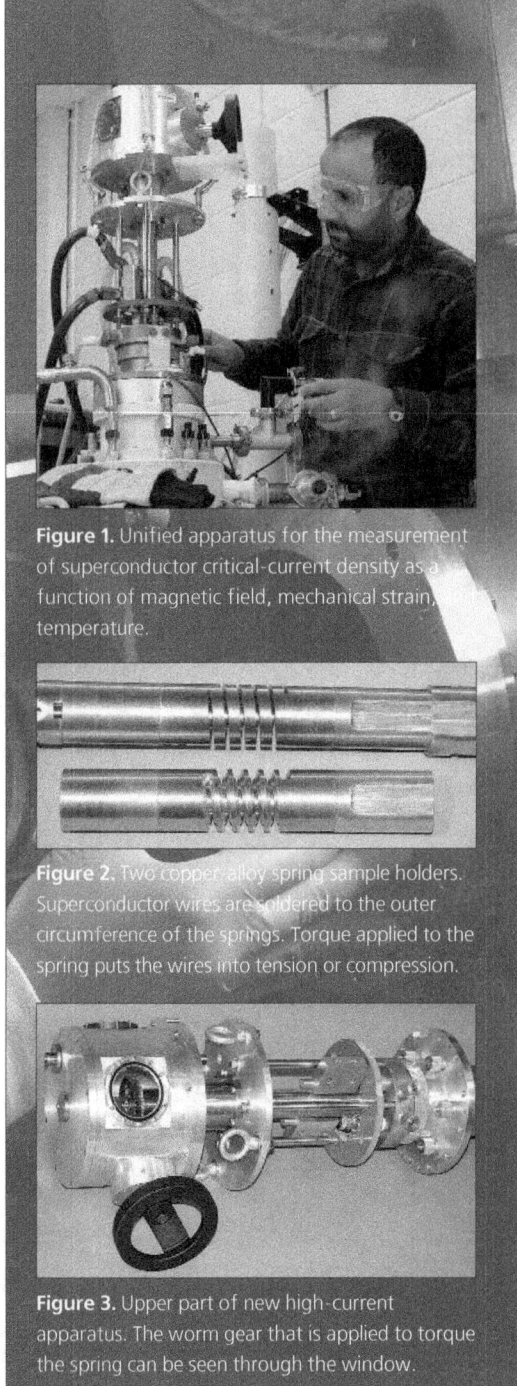

Figure 1. Unified apparatus for the measurement of superconductor critical-current density as a function of magnetic field, mechanical strain, and temperature.

Figure 2. Two copper-alloy spring sample holders. Superconductor wires are soldered to the outer circumference of the springs. Torque applied to the spring puts the wires into tension or compression.

Figure 3. Upper part of new high-current apparatus. The worm gear that is applied to torque the spring can be seen through the window.

Contact

Loren Goodrich

(303) 497-3143

loren.goodrich@nist.gov

www.ingramcontent.com/pod-product-compliance
Lightning Source LLC
Chambersburg PA
CBHW052005280526
45793CB00005B/855